Maria Anne Hirschmann
and Betty Pershing

FOLLOW ME

BOOKS

S.P.A.R.C. PUBLISHING COMPANY
HUNTINGTON BEACH, CALIFORNIA 92648

Scripture quotations in this publication are primarily the author's paraphrase. Bible versions quoted are the following:
RSV From the RSV of the Bible, copyrighted 1946 and 1952 by the division of Christian Education of the NCCC, U.S.A., and used by permission.
TLB From *The Living Bible*, Copyright © 1971 by Tyndale House Publishers, Wheaton, Illinois. Used by permission.
KJV The Authorized King James Version.

© Copyright 1979 by Maria Anne Hirschmann, Hansi Ministries, Inc.
Huntington Beach, CA 92648 All rights reserved.

Published by S.P.A.R.C. Publishing Company
for Hansi Ministries, Inc.
Huntington Beach, California 92648
Printed in U.S.A.

Library of Congress Catalog Card No. 79-84331
ISBN 0-932878-01-6

CONTENTS

Introduction **6**
1. Before the Beginnings **11**
2. The Chosen People **16**
3. God's Timing **21**
4. Like a Little Lamb **26**
5. The Young Child **30**
6. At the Age of Twelve **35**
7. Years of Preparation **41**
8. This *Is* My Beloved Son **47**
9. Satan Tries! **52**
10. Follow Me **60**
11. Toward Human Dignity **66**
12. A Chance to Believe **72**
13. Jesus Sees the Heart **80**
14. A Prophet in His Own Country **89**
15. Jesus Came to Heal **96**
16. Jesus Came to Bring Life **104**
17. Jesus Came to Meet Human Needs **116**
18. Jesus Came to Cleanse and Drive Out Demons **129**
19. The Father Glorifies His Son **138**
20. Hosanna to the Son of David **146**
21. What Does the Future Hold? **156**
22. A Farewell Dinner **165**
23. Friend—How Can You Do This? **174**
24. Crucify Him! **183**
25. It Is Finished! **192**
26. Follow Only Me **207**
Bibliography **223**

INTRODUCTION

Every land and time has its own culture, customs and habits. Even the children of different countries play different games.

When I came as an immigrant to America I had to learn to understand many new words and things. Until I grasped the meaning of some of the strange habits my American neighbors displayed I often felt rebuffed and alienated. When I began to understand what they said and why they did what they did, I began to feel at home. Understanding brings acquiescence and communication.

My two small children learned and adjusted with greater ease than I did. English fast became their mother tongue. Soon they too played the games our neighbor children played.

One of the new games I watched them play was "Follow the Leader." They loved to copy and outguess each other. They tried to anticipate every move the leader made. They laughed and squeeled when they managed to stay in the game in spite of some unexpected moves. They tried again in another game if they were outtricked and had to quit. It was fun!

The game intrigued me. I did much thinking about it. I watched my children play it and realized how often the children of God play a similar game, but with much less laughter and enjoyment.

We see ourselves in a long line behind our leader, the Lord Jesus Christ. We try so hard to follow Him because He told us to do so. We try to outguess His moves and often we don't see Him clearly enough to know what He does. So we stumble off His designed path or run ahead of Him. We foul everything up and quit the game. After awhile we ask for a rerun and try to do better—but we always end up defeated. It's no fun! It's no game either; it is for real!

When Jesus turned to His disciples and said, "Follow Me," He had no child's play in mind. It was a way of life, the *only* way of life.

His rules are also different. He, as our leader, does not try to out-trick us. His form and way are not mysterious and hard to figure out. We can *know* His intentions and plans for our lives.

As babes in Christ we may have a hard time at first to see Him and His leading very clearly. This is normal. A baby has to grow into understanding and knowledge and this takes time. How often we misunderstand Him. We play childish games with Him and others. We even think that we are "out of the game" every time we make a wrong move. We ask to be born again every time we miss a mark. We wonder if we are still children of the heavenly Father because we goofed or fell down. We are afraid to get up and try again. What a pity! How sad we make God's heart when we feel so unsure and insecure.

Jesus is eager for us to *know* Him and understand His dealing with us. He wants us to understand everything about Him and the other two persons of the Godhead, the Father and the Holy Spirit. The better we know Him the easier it will be for us to be His followers. Jesus never intended to make salvation a funny or fearful guessing game; He came to this earth to *reveal* God and His will. He lived and walked with men to *show* us His Father's character and love. He didn't come to force us to follow Him in a bewildering fog where we can see only a dim outline. He came to be God-with-us that we may see Him as a human reality.

The more we know Jesus, the more we will love Him. The more we fall in love with Him, the more we *want* to follow Him. The more we want to follow Him, the easier it is to know His will and leading. To know Him is to trust Him!

This book is written to help babes in Christ become acquainted with Jesus in the cultural settings He lived in while here on earth. Much research about the Jewish and Roman culture in Christ's time has preceded these lessons.

The more we know about the customs and habits Christ lived with, the better we comprehend the pictures of the language He used, and the more we will be at ease with Him and His Word, the Bible.

What we don't know or understand makes us afraid. My children and I were terribly afraid of America and the American people in the beginning. As we lived in this land and became familiar with the culture and the language, we fell in love with both the country and her people.

It is our great hope that this Bible study will help many babes in Christ to fall in love with the person and life of Jesus Christ. One book can *never* show all there is to know, for a thousand books could never tell the whole story of Him. This is only a beginning. Many volumes have already been written on the life and teachings of Jesus Christ. Many more will be written. Yet, none of them can or will ever say *all* there is to say about Him.

We don't attempt to rewrite what has been written already. All this book tries to do is to make His story so simple that even babes may see Him—and see Him as He really was and is!

Jesus became like one of us. He became human that He might *know* us: our temptations, our sorrows, our joys, our lives and our deaths. He knows everything there is to know about you and me—but how much do we know about Him?

Let's meet Him together!

How to Use This Book

You have a choice! There are several options you may exercise in the use of this book:

1. Read it as a story of Jesus' life. You will learn much and find enjoyment and challenge in the material.

2. Read the book slowly with a Bible close by. Look up the Scriptures. Re-read each chapter several times. Since there are twenty-six chapters, you can spread out your reading for six months.

3. For maximum benefit, get the study guide that is prepared for *Follow Me*. Each day do one of the sections in the guide, read this book and look up all Scriptures. Let the message invade and become a part of you. Determine what Jesus wants to tell you about His life and your life.

Get together with some friends and study together. Compare what each of you writes in the study guide. You can have a Bible class with or without a teacher. Sharing your ideas and reviewing the book and the Scripture texts will provide you with authority for your learning.

Whichever option you choose, be sure to read and then to pray the prayers at the end of each chapter. These are patterns to help you learn to talk to God. Prayer is the breathing of the Christian's spirit. It need not be formal or follow a specified form—just talk to God as you talk to your friend. For additional help in communicating with God and listening to Him, see chapters 15,16,17,39, and 40 in the book, *I Am But a Child in Christ*.[1]

As you read this book you will notice an abundance of background and cultural material. The New Testament was written about two thousand years ago in a world and culture quite different from ours. To really understand the subtleties of what was going on and what Jesus was saying, we need to transport ourselves into that history, culture and thinking. The facts will help accomplish the first two, but it will take some doing on our part to accomplish the last—the thinking.

The Greek, Roman and our thinking might be described as analytical and precise. If we say yesterday, we mean one day ago. To us a son is one generation away from his father. A number is a precise means of counting.

The Jewish mind didn't work that way. Yesterday could mean a generation away or it could mean one day. Time is not measured so exactly. "Son of" could mean the son of a father, or the grandson, or even a distant descendent. Numbers are often used as symbols; for example, forty years is one generation, seven may be a symbol for completeness. And so on and on.

When we try to put our scientific way of thinking into the conceptual world of the Bible people, we find ourselves in difficulty. Every attempt has been made in the writing of this book to help you think like one who lived in the Middle East. Make a conscious effort to enter the world of the first century and to walk today where and when and how Jesus walked. Ask Jesus to help you understand Him. He will do it if you let Him!

Footnote

1. Maria Anne Hirschmann, *I Am But a Child in Christ* (Huntington Beach, CA: Hansi Ministries, Inc., 1977).

1
BEFORE THE BEGINNINGS

In the beginning was God (John 1:1). God *was*! That means He existed before any of the beginnings we know of. God is eternal or pre-existing (Psalm 90:2). Some people have a hard time with this concept. They try to understand what it means and stumble over it, instead of accepting it by faith.

We humans will have to understand our own limitations first in order to accept God's pre-existence. Because sin destroyed the eternal dimension for the human race, we can no longer comprehend with our mind. A born-again person reaches for the concept of an eternal God by faith. We believe it because we trust God and we know that we shall be able to understand some things in eternity, where we will be like Him and see Him as He is (1 John 3:2; 1 Corinthians 13:12).

Christ was with God always (John 1:1,2). We do not know in what form He existed before He came to this earth, but we know that through Him *all* things were made (John 1:3). He is the Creator and life-giver (John 1:4). The Father ordained His only Son to execute His will and plans for the whole universe (Colossians 1:15-17).

The Bible records mainly the things pertaining to our globe. It's an earthbook and it tells the story of and for the human race. It gives God's plan of salvation in the setting of a great conflict between good and evil here on earth alone.

What happened elsewhere in the universe or how the great controversy between God and the evil force began are told only in snatches in the Bible. We find parts here and there as they influence human history. Bible students can fit the various pieces together, like a puzzle, into a pattern; when we complete it we have a pretty good idea what happened before our world began.

In case you have not studied about the "Origin of Evil" in *I Am But a Child in Christ*,[1] or in some other Bible study, let's review it briefly. We must first understand what happened before the foundation of the earth was laid that we may then understand *why* Jesus Christ, the Son of God, came to this earth to live with us as a human being.

It all began when God contemplated the creation of creatures. He had to make a decision. Would He create beings who would worship and obey Him like robots—machines that He turned on or wound up like a music box? Or would He create beings who had a free will, a freedom of choice to worship God because they loved Him enough to want to worship Him?

God is love and love cannot be served by force—ever! (See 1 John 4:8; 1 Peter 5:1,2.) God chose to create beings who were free to choose for themselves. They could love Him or turn against Him, as one beautiful angel named Lucifer did. He turned against God (Isaiah 14:12-14; Ezekiel 28:14,15). He started a war in heaven and seduced one-third of God's children, the angels. He became Satan and he and the rebellious forces were cast out of heaven (Revelation 12:7-9; see also 1 Peter 2:9; Jude 6). Satan rebelled because he wanted to be like God (Isaiah 14:12-14). When he was thrown out of heaven, he looked for a kingdom where he would be a "god." Our earth looked like a very fine place for his schemes.

Adam and Eve had received the same great gift of freedom of choice that the angels had before them. They were children of God, made in the likeness of God (Genesis 1:26,27). They were permitted to think and do as they willed. They could choose either to obey and trust and worship God or turn against Him (Genesis 2:16,17).

When Eve was seduced by the serpent and Adam chose to disobey God, sin and sorrow came to the earth (Genesis 3:6,7). Sin brings death (Romans 6:23). God knew that. He made everything, even the laws for the universe and our earth. So, if God created everything, did He *create* evil, sin and doubt?

No, He did not create such things, He allowed them as a possibility. In order to give mankind freedom of choice He had to do so. How can anyone choose unless he has more than one option to chose from? Even though God knew that the wrong desire of His children would bring evil into His beautiful new world, He permitted it. Freedom of choice is so important to God that He took the risk. What risk? That He would pay the price for giving such a great gift!

When God laid the plans for our earth in great wisdom, He foresaw the possibility of Adam's fall. He did not ordain that it should happen, but He, being all-knowing, prepared for the terrible emergency when it would happen.

The Son of God, our Creator, took the responsibility for the earth creatures He would make. If they chose to sin, He would die in their place.

The plan of salvation, the life and death of Jesus Christ were not an afterthought. After sin occurred and Adam sold out to Satan, God didn't quickly formulate a battle plan to begin another war on earth. Rather,

God's love had designed the redemption story before He laid the foundation of the earth. The Lamb was slain when love decided to give freedom of choice (Revelation 13:8). God finally revealed "the mystery which hath been kept in silence through times eternal" (Romans 16:25).

Think of it! The Son of God *knew* that He would die on the earth when He created it. His hands made the tree He would be nailed to! His breath put the spark of life into the human form who would sell Him out to Satan. He created the couple who would be His very own ancestors, and also the ancestors of those who would kill Him in blind hatred someday.

Can we comprehend such love? When the earth came from the hand of our Creator, everything was perfect (Genesis 1:31). Bright sunlight smiled under a deep blue sky upon the earth; gentle slopes were covered with deep green grass, beautiful flowers and blooming trees; lakes and rivers were filled with crystal clear water. Tame animals roamed in the Garden of Eden and God's two new children rejoiced with the other creatures God had created before them (Job 38:4-7).

Everything Christ made spoke of one thing *only*, His Father's love. The Son of God knows only *one* desire: He wants to reveal His Father's glory and be His image. He reflected His Father when He made the earth. He showered His Father's love in a greater measure when He came to redeem it. How can anyone help but love and adore Him as we see the glory of God in the face of Jesus Christ? (See 2 Corinthians 4:6.)

LET'S PRAY: Dear Father in heaven, my soul fails to grasp the scope of Your love and the freedom You have given me. I cannot even comprehend why my freedom of choice was so important to You that Your Son was willing to die for it—to set me free again.

As I contemplate the life and death of Christ, teach me through Your Holy Spirit that I might see Him more clearly—for to see and to know Him means to love Him.

I want to love you Father through Jesus Your Son. Amen.

Footnote

1. Maria Anne Hirschmann, *I Am But a Child in Christ* (Huntington Beach, CA: Hansi Ministries, Inc., 1977).

2
THE CHOSEN PEOPLE

God revealed His plan of salvation to Adam and Eve in the Garden of Eden. He promised a Saviour in their darkest hour of despair, right after they had sinned (Genesis 3:15). He gave them a worship ritual that would remind them of the Lamb of God who would someday come to earth and die for them.

It seems our first parents looked for a fulfillment of God's promise in their lifetime. They received their firstborn son with joy for they called him *Cain*, which means "I have gotten a man, *the Lord*." What a heartbreak to them that he turned out to be the first murderer instead of the deliverer. Their son Abel, though God-fearing, was not the expected one either. He died as the first martyr for he irritated his brother by his right and pure form of worship (Genesis 4:4).

When another son was born (Genesis 4:25), his parents called him *Seth*, the "appointed one" or "substitute." They still hoped for the man who would restore Eden to them. But Adam and Eve died without seeing the fulfillment of God's promise during their long lifetime.

As soon as Satan became the "god" on earth (and as the families multiplied and spread across the earth) two distinct groups began to form. Some families and tribes followed God and believed His promise even though He delayed His return to earth. The rest followed Satan and their own corrupted flesh (Genesis 6:5-12).

From the days of Enoch, by patriarchs and prophets, the promise of God was repeated and handed down from generation to generation. Hope kindled in many mothers' hearts when they held a newborn son in their arms. The flood nearly extinguished all hope, but one family survived to carry the seed and the promise (Genesis 7:1).

That family also multiplied, and the centuries passed. God found Himself a man who would become the father of a special people; the man was Abram (Genesis 12:1, 2). Bible scholars put Abram approximately two thousand years before the birth of Jesus Christ. Abram waited not only for a Saviour and a city whose builder was God (Hebrews 11:8-10), he had to wait most of his life for a son, the seed who would carry on God's promise (Genesis 15:2-6).

But God had given Abram a promise: "I will bless thee," the Lord said, "and in thee shall *all* the families of the earth be blessed" (Genesis 12:2,3). And God changed his name to Abraham which means "father of a multitude" (Genesis 17:5).

God *never* breaks a promise but He is not bound by our time to keep it. God has His own timing and a thousand years are to Him like a day and a day as a thousand years (2 Peter 3:8).

God showed Abraham that his descendents would be in Egypt for more than four hundred years. Then they would return and inherit the land of Canaan (Genesis 15:13-16).

To Abraham's seed, the people of Israel, God gave His prophecies about the Messiah and His laws. He designed their ritual services, (Genesis 49:10; Leviticus 22:31-33; 23:4), every part of which pointed to Christ and had deep spiritual significance (Hebrews 9:11,12). But the Israelites were slow to learn.

In the wilderness they murmured and complained

(Exodus 14:11; 15:24; 16:2). When they entered the land of Canaan, they forgot God's purpose for them as a special nation. They had been chosen by God to be a light and a "wise and understanding people" to the rest of the world (Deuteronomy 4:6; see also Deuteronomy 26:19; 28:10). Instead of leading and teaching the other nations, they followed the satanic ways of the heathen. God sent them many warnings through the prophets; He allowed them to suffer heathen oppression, famine and adversity, which they brought upon themselves by their disobedience. The Old Testament is full of tragic reports where God's chosen people repented, had a short reformation, then fell into deeper apostasy.

Israel's prime time was under King David and King Solomon, just about one thousand years before Jesus was born. Four hundred years later most of the Jewish people found themselves under subjection and living in Babylon. The city of Jerusalem and the Temple had been destroyed. Homesick, they mourned for the holy Temple and longed to go back to Jerusalem (Psalm 137).

After seventy years God permitted them to return (Jeremiah 25:11). Ezra and Nehemiah were key figures in the restoration of Jerusalem and the Temple (Nehemiah 6:1-3; 8:5,6).

As heathen oppression continued the Jews came to the conclusion that their prosperity depended upon their obedience to the Torah (the five books of Moses or the Law). After they returned from Babylon, the people began to build synagogues where the Law was taught by rabbis and scribes. Schools were established to teach both children and adults.

But the people tried to keep the laws of the Torah for the wrong motives. They hoped to accomplish the wrong things. They believed that keeping every little Mosaic rule and law would bring them greater wealth and worldly acclaim and free them again to become an independent nation. They did not do the things of God because they loved Him but in order to try to force His favor. The worship rules became ends in themselves. They did not point anymore to the One who ordained them. The people put their trust in the symbolic ceremony, not in God Himself. Any worship of God became empty ritual.

So the priests and scribes began to fill the void by multiplying the requirements of keeping the Law. The more rigid and demanding the Law-keeping was made, the harder the people tried to "earn" God's favor and the more they lost their spiritual insight and true vision.

When motives are not in the right place and God is served for reasons other than love, everything is out of balance. The Jewish nation got farther and farther off center and suffered much persecution. They tried to improve their lot by interpreting the Torah in more complexity and greater detail. But it was of no avail.

The Greeks nearly destroyed Jerusalem and the Jews about three hundred years before Christ's birth. The conquerors tried to Hellenize the whole world of that time—to force everybody to become Greeks and speak their language. The Jews rebelled and fought for their survival.

About sixty years before Jesus came to earth, the Romans had conquered both the Southern and the Northern kingdoms of Israel. Rome did not push the Jews as far as the Greeks had. Even though they called the entire known world of that time "The Roman Empire," the Romans did not try to force Roman culture on the other nations. The Jews were permitted to maintain their own national culture and worship. But they hated the Roman oppressors with a passion. Rome exacted from them their money and demanded their submission which for a true Jew was harder to give than money.

By the time the birth of Christ drew near the Jewish nation was in a terrible condition. The priests and scribes had increased the demands of the Law-keeping to the point where it was nearly impossible to keep all the Law. Even those who longed with all their heart to serve God labored so under the heavy burden of trying to keep all the Law that they could not find rest for their troubled souls. Their conscience accused them day and night.

The priesthood itself was corrupt. The Romans reserved for themselves the right to appoint the high priest. The position was bought by much money. Fraud, bribery, greed, violence, frequent revolts and distrust poisoned the national life. Spiritual ignorance and apathy had settled into most people's heart.

Had Satan and his forces triumphed again? The world was covered with darkness and the knowledge of the true God had nearly been wiped out.

And into that deep darkness God shed a light—and the darkness could not overcome it, ever!

LET'S PRAY: Dear God, it seems so hard to understand how Your own chosen people could be so confused and hardened in their understanding of Your loving plans for this world.

Show me if I need some softening of my heart too—and if so, break it open by Your Spirit. Don't let me depend on anything or anybody but on Jesus.

Help me to know that neither law-keeping nor good works will save me—Christ alone can. Amen.

3
GOD'S TIMING

"When the fulness of the time was come, God sent forth His Son ... to redeem them that were under the law" (Galatians 4:4,5). God knows no haste nor delay in His planning. Like the stars are placed by His command and everything in the universe runs precisely at its appointed time, so God knew exactly the right hour and the place His Son would have to be born.

God began to lay His plans long before the actual moment arrived. As we have learned, the coming of God's Son was planned before the foundation of the earth was laid. Through the ages God spoke of it through His prophets and kings: Daniel revealed the time of His arrival (Daniel 9:24-26); Micah gave the name of the place where He would be born (Micah 5:2); David received God's promise that his seed would be established forever (2 Samuel 7:16). The Son of David had to be born in the city of David—where King David was born— Bethlehem (1 Samuel 16:1).

Though the scrolls of prophecy were available for the priests and scribes, very few searched them with a longing heart. The hope for the Messiah was alive only in the hearts of very few people. Among these few were the priest, Zacharias and his wife, Elizabeth. This old and God-fearing couple without children received the announcement of Christ's soon coming and, amidst special signs and miracles, had been chosen to become the parents of the Messiah's forerunner (Luke 1:13-17).

Then came the special moment when the angel Gabriel visited a virgin named Mary (Luke 1:26-33). In this very well-known story it is obvious that Mary was greatly honored by God. Wasn't she fortunate? There is no doubt that God honored her by entrusting the little baby Jesus to her care. But it is not so sure that she was honored by the people she lived with. Just the opposite is much more in order for her time.

Let's look at the customs of Christ's time to understand what a special woman Mary must have been when she willingly said to the angel: "Be it unto me according to thy word" (Luke 1:38). Mary, a virgin, was betrothed to Joseph. Both came from the royal line of David. Betrothal was a marriage contract made by the prospective bridegroom and the bride's father. Most of the time the father received a sum of money for his daughter. We do not know what arrangements were made in Mary's case since her parents are never mentioned in the Bible.

Tradition tells us that Joseph was a widower with children from his previous marriage. If that is so, it was not in harmony with the customs of that day. The Jewish community frowned upon large age differences in couples. The usual age of betrothal for a Jewish girl was twelve to twelve-and-a-half years. The twelfth birthday marked the change from childhood to youth in the life of both boys and girls. The age of marriage for a young man ranged from sixteen years to twenty-four years of age. But it was an embarrassment to the boy if he wasn't married by the popular age of twenty.

After the betrothal, which was celebrated by drinking a glass of wine together while a special benediction was said over it, the two people became husband and wife. The groom then went back to his father's house to prepare himself for the marriage feast. The preparation usually took twelve months. Then the groom, escorted by a procession of his friends, would go to the bride's house. He would claim his bride and bring her and her attendants to his home for the wedding feast. During this feast they entered the bridal chamber to consummate the marriage.

If a girl was found pregnant during the time of separation, it was a cause of great shame. If the betrothed husband did not acknowledge the child as his own, he could punish the unfaithful woman in several ways. He either could send her back to her parents without returning the dowery, put her away (divorce her) or she could be punished by death through stoning.

Mary was in the twelve-month separation period, waiting for Joseph to come and get her. She was a virgin, for the wedding feast had not yet taken place. It never did take place! When that precious young teenage girl said "Be it unto me according to thy word," she stepped by faith on a long hard road which finally led to a cross.

As soon as Mary knew that she would have God's child she went to visit her cousin Elizabeth who was six months pregnant. Both women *knew* that God was doing something very special (Luke 1:39-56).

After three months Mary returned to her own house and her body began to show some changes. When Joseph found out about her pregnancy, he was deeply troubled. He loved her enough that he didn't want her to be stoned so he decided to put her away quietly. After all he was a man of good reputation (Matthew 1:19).

We don't know if Mary ever got to him to tell him what really happened. The couple could only see each other chaperoned during the year of separation, and the girl had to wear a veil. Maybe she did whisper it to him, but it was just too hard to believe.

So God sent an angel to Joseph also who explained things very plainly (Matthew 1:18-25). Mary must have been very precious in God's eyes, and so was Joseph. Joseph loved God and his wife enough that he was willing to take gossip and embarrassment though he hadn't done anything wrong.

There was no marriage feast! He took his wife without any special ceremony quietly into his house. And they never entered the marriage chamber until after the child was born.

Close to the time of the baby's birth, the Roman emperor sent special orders that everyone in his empire had to be taxed. Everyone had to go and register in what we would call today his county seat or the district according to the tribe to which he belonged. Joseph and Mary came from the tribe of Judah, so they had to make a long journey from Nazareth in Galilee to Bethlehem in Judea (Luke 2:1-5).

Under normal circumstances such a trip might have taken them two weeks. Since Jews didn't cross Samaria, the people traveled at least 120 miles from Nazareth, across the Jordon River down through Perea and into Judea. Ten miles a day took much effort and sweat. It was the custom to travel in caravans or groups. Lone travelers were in danger of being robbed or assaulted by hostile non-Jews.

We don't know if Mary rode a donkey; only well-to-do people could afford such luxury. Maybe she walked and carried herself slowly as she was heavy with child. It was hard to keep up with the others. She had to rest every so often and the going got slower and slower.

When they finally arrived, it was night and the little town of Bethlehem was overcrowded with people. Bethlehem was not set up for tourists. It was such an insignificant, small, peasant place that it didn't even have a city wall. Maybe the whole town had only one inn. And the inn was full.

If Joseph had been rich he could have bribed his way into a house somewhere, but he wasn't. He was a poor carpenter who had lost many days wages because the

Roman emperor got a whim to tax his subjects some more.

Wouldn't it have been easier and better if God had intervened and the child could have been born in their home in Nazareth? God *did* intervene and the emperor, Caesar Augustus, was used by God though he didn't know it. God's Son *must* be born in the right place for the sake of Jewish tradition—and at the right time.

Joseph bedded down his young teenage wife in a stable on stubble and straw—and that night the Saviour was born!

LET'S PRAY: Dear Father in heaven, it must have been hard for Your Father's heart to let Your only Son leave heaven so that He might come and be with us. You *gave* Your Son, didn't you? And you never got Him back the way He was before He left heaven. How I thank You for Your great and unselfish love. And how I thank You, Jesus, for Your willingness to come like a little lamb. I love You both. Amen.

4
LIKE A LITTLE LAMB

I wonder what Mary thought when she laid her newborn Son into a crude manger. Everything was dirty around her. After all it was a place for animals, not for people. Mary knew that the baby would be born while she was away from home so she brought oil, salt and swaddling clothes for the occasion. Swaddling clothes were strips of simple linen which were used to wrap both newborn babies and people who had died.

A newborn child was first cleaned with water and oil and rubbed with salt (Ezekiel 16:4), then wrapped tightly with those special strips of cloth. The baby remained swaddled for the first seven days. After that the child received its first bath.

I am glad for Mary's sake that this was the custom. What would she have done if she had to bathe Him right away? What did she think when the child, conceived by the Holy Spirit (Luke 1:35) and announced by an angel both to her and Joseph (Matthew 1:20-23; Luke 1:26-35), had to see the light of this world in a smelly, dirty and cold stable? Did she wonder for a moment if all the things that had happened in the last nine months of her life were only a dream?

Why would God let His royal Son be born in such a humble place, under unhygenic, forbidding and even dangerous conditions? Why was He born like a little lamb in a stable? Wouldn't the baby catch a cold or an infection? Couldn't Mary get sick and not be able to nurse the child? Why would God do such a thing *if* He were in control?

God *was* in control. His Son had to be born so lowly and humble that nobody could ever claim that Christ lived His life on this earth spoiled and pampered. He had to share humanity on its lowest and rawest level right from the beginning. Because of it, He would be able to understand human suffering, poverty and rejection and be able to comfort anyone who would come to Him while He lived on earth and after He left again (Hebrews 2:17,18).

We can be sure that all heaven and the universe watched in breathless excitement as the baby was born and took His first deep breath!

Nobody knows how the transition took place. The Bible does not tell us how it happened. We know that the Son of God *left* heaven to come to us (John 6:38). The Bible does not tell us in what form He existed before He came to us. All we know is that God is a Spirit (John 4:24).

Somewhere in this whole happening there came a moment when Christ handed the sceptre of His rulership to His Father. He walked out of heaven's gate and the door closed behind Him. He came down to our dark, cold, sin-sick planet as a helpless little babe and entrusted Himself to two creatures He Himself had created. He came to a place that was ruled by an evil, powerful being called Satan. A being who hated God with all his might. He would therefore also hate the child born of God and do his utmost to destroy Him.

Can anyone ever comprehend the love of God? (See Romans 5:5-8; 8:35-39; Ephesians 3:14-19.)

Angels marveled and desired to look into the great mystery of God's salvation (1 Peter 1:12). Angels must have also marveled and been aghast at the indifference the Jewish people displayed when God finally stooped down and came to live with His created beings.

What an hour of joy! What a time for singing! Whenever the angelic hosts are happy, they long to sing and shout and glorify God (Luke 2:13,14;15:7). The heavens were ready to burst with joy and praise and anxious to announce the good news. Eagerly, the angels who had drawn near to earth to watch the beautiful sight, looked for someone to tell what they couldn't contain any longer.

Wasn't there *anybody* who would listen? To hear angels one must not only listen with the ears but with the heart. Were there no hearts left anywhere who waited for the Redeemer and longed for Him?

In the fields where once the boy David had watched his flock, shepherds were keeping their sheep that night. Only in the wintertime would the shepherds bring their sheep to the fields of Bethlehem. In the summer they would trek up to Galilee. The south offers warmth and pasture in the winter. When the winter rains stop, the sheep must go north where there is green pasture and more food. Seasons and weather cycles determine the places where sheep and shepherds stay. Through the long and silent hours of the night the sheep had to be watched. Did the shepherds talk about the Messiah that night? Did they pray? Did they sing softly around a little camp fire?

The angel of the Lord came to the shepherds that night and the glory of God lit the darkness. He told them the beautiful news and quieted their fears. After their human eyes had gotten used to such heavenly brightness, the rest of the angels couldn't hold back any longer. They *had* to burst out in song and heaven and earth flooded with heavenly glory, joy and music (Luke 2:9-14).

When the hills of Bethlehem quieted down again and night settled once more over the land, the shepherds decided to go and find the newborn babe. In the dawn of a new day they found Him and glorified and praised

God. They told everybody what God had told them—and Mary listened carefully. She tucked it all away in her heart and I am sure it comforted her greatly (Luke 2:19).

As she listened to the story of the shepherds she knew again what she had known all along: this *was* God's Son and God hadn't forsaken them after all. He *knew* they were in a stable: Mary, Joseph and a little boy who would be called, Jesus, as soon as He was eight days old (Luke 2:21).

Jesus was the Greek name for the Hebrew name, *Joshua*. Every Jew knew what the name meant: Saviour. The Jews longed for a saviour to save them from heathen oppression. But God said, "He shall save His people from their *sins*" (Matthew 1:21)!

Nobody understood fully what God intended to do. The shepherds rejoiced that the deliverer had come. Mary looked at Him with fond ambitious dreams toward human greatness—and the newborn Son of God slept and cried when He was hungry and cuddled in His mother's arms—just like any other little baby. How tiny! How human! How precious He was—sweet like a little innocent lamb!

LET'S PRAY: Dear Jesus, the true Christmas story boggles my mind. When I look at the nativity scene as we picture it every year, it all looks so clean and neat and special.

It was special all right, but it wasn't very clean or warm when You arrived, was it? Germs and cold night air, poverty and no bed to lay Your little head—and nobody cared enough to let You come into his home. I wonder, would *I* have welcomed You in? Help me to open the door of my heart and house to You—and to others who need my help. Let me love for Thy sake. Amen.

5
THE YOUNG CHILD

We do not know how long Joseph had to keep his young wife and her new Babe in the stable. As the registration was completed and the extra taxes were paid, people left hurriedly to get back to work and to their own homes. The little family stayed behind.

When Jesus was eight days old, Joseph took his and Mary's firstborn Son to be circumcised and they gave Him the name Jesus. It was a very common name. Many mothers had called their sons by that name, hoping that he would be the deliverer and saviour of Israel. Whenever any Jew thought of deliverence or the need of a saviour, he would think of the restoration of a full Jewish nation. It was a national virtue to hate the Romans and to look for political freedom and new power and fame (John 11:47, 48).

Full of spiritual and national pride, the priests strictly enforced all the detailed laws and rules of their worship rituals. Every respectable Jew adhered to those rules. Joseph was a decent and good citizen (Matthew 1:19) and he did everything according to the Mosaic and the priestly laws. One of those laws, circumcision, began with Abraham and was a sign that God had a special covenant with Abraham's seed (Genesis 17:11).

Mary was not allowed to attend Jesus' circumcision ceremony because she had to go through a forty-day purification after Jesus' birth, during which time she could not enter the sanctuary (Leviticus 12:2-4). A woman was considered unclean for forty days when she gave birth to a boy and sixty-six days when she delivered a girl (Leviticus 12:2-8).

Forty days after Jesus' birth Mary and Joseph took Him to Jerusalem for the dedication ceremony. The firstborn son had to be redeemed from God by five shekels of silver (Numbers 18:16) since every firstborn of man and beast belonged to Him (Exodus 13:13). The mother of the child had to bring a sacrifice of a lamb for a burnt offering and a young pigeon or turtledove for a sin offering. If the parents were too poor, two turtledoves or pigeons could be accepted (Leviticus 12:8).

The priest most likely didn't even look up when two peasants in Galilean clothing walked up to bring their humble sacrifice. He held the little boy before the altar in a dedication ceremony without much thought. So many children were dedicated in the Temple; unless the parents were famous or wealthy and could make his work worthwhile with a special gift, why bother?

But God saw to it that His Son's dedication ceremony did not go completely unrecognized. He sent two special witnesses! Simeon, an old man of high reputation entered the Temple just as little Jesus was dedicated. The Holy Spirit had promised that devout and faithful man that he should not see death until he had seen the Lord's Christ. Simeon poured his jubilant heart out while he held Mary's son in his arms.

I wonder if the priest listened? We know that Joseph and Mary did. They marveled at Simeon's words (Luke 2:25-32). I am sure that Mary must have recalled the old man's words often at a later time when the going got very rough!

Anna, a very old prophetess, confirmed Simeon's words and also praised the Lord for the Redeemer and Lord in the form of a little boy (Luke 2:36-38).

Scripture tells us several things that our Christmas

tradition ignores. For example, Joseph and Mary found a little house in Bethlehem and settled there to live for a while. We know this because when the wise men came from the East to find Jesus and worship Him, they came into a house and looking for the young child (Matthew 2:11). The Jewish term, "young child," applies to a toddler, not a babe. Jesus could have been a year or older when the famous visitors came. The Bible also does not tell us that only three wise men came. We know only that they brought three special gifts. It is more likely that a whole caravan came, for even simple travelers were in great danger of being robbed, and what the wise men carried was worth taking. They carried gifts for a king or high dignitary (Matthew 2:11).

Gold is the gift for a king. Frankincense is used in worship and is a gift of high price. Myrrh is one of the spices used for burial. It was an Eastern custom to give a baby the first precious ointments or spices for his death. People gathered these spices all their lives for their preparation to be buried. They often put a lifesavings into rare aromatic spices and herbs which would subdue the odor of the decaying body.

We don't know too much about the wise men. The Bible gives only a few verses of that story. As we read between the lines we cannot help but wonder, "Did the wise men know why they brought what they brought?" God had ordained His Son to be King of kings, our High Priest and the Saviour of the world. We know that the wise men followed a star. Somehow they must have read about the star "out of Jacob" (Numbers 24:17). How the Hebrew Scriptures got to them nobody knows.

We are aware that many Jews remained in Babylon, people who stayed true to their race and traditions. It could easily be that their ancient prophecies were carried to the far East, like Persia and other lands. Since the Jews were merchants who traveled far and wide, God's holy Word was spread throughout heathen countries. God intended it that way. It was the Jew's interpretation of God's Word, back home in Israel, that kept them from letting God's light shine in the world's darkness.

God had warned the Jews not to mix and associate with idolaters (Deuteronomy 7:1-5), but the Jews interpreted this to mean becoming completely separated from the rest of the world. They actually took it as an insult if God showed mercy to any Gentiles. When the wise men arrived in Jerusalem, they caused much excitement. They obviously had very limited information for they didn't even know the place of birth of the newborn King (Matthew 2:2).

Herod did some careful listening and showed great interest in what *time* the star had first appeared (Matthew 2:7). From this he calculated carefully and figured that if he killed every child two years and under he would destroy the Christ child (Matthew 2:16).

Before Herod's soldiers came to execute his inhuman orders, an angel wakened Joseph and told him to take the young Child and His mother to Egypt. There wasn't much time for packing! It would take them at least two weeks to make the trip. As poor as they were how would they pay for such a long journey?

Did the Gentile wise men of the East come only to worship this newborn king? Did they not also come to stir up Jerusalem and draw the attention of the leaders and priests to an overlooked event and encourage them to study the Hebrew prophecies again? Did God use them to bring death and heartbreak to mothers by their innocent inquiry? (History tells us that about twenty male children were slaughtered.)

Yes, God used the wise men for all of these reasons—and for more!

It is most likely that the gifts the wise men gave to the parents of the little child Jesus were sold and the money used to sustain life for all three of them while they traveled and lived in Egypt. Nowhere in the Bible record of Christ's life are those gifts ever mentioned again. He had no ointments or spices of His own when He died. He never owned any gold or frankincense to finance His ministry.

The wise men departed and went back to their own country and they might never have understood and known all there was to know. They came and went. They brought themselves and their gifts on a journey of more than a thousand miles and many long weary months to see a little peasant child. They gave the gifts of adoration and love and left on the long, long journey back home.

God used them and their gifts as He saw fit. God will *always* use what is given in love by wise men who seek Him, even now!

LET'S PRAY: Father, I am so glad You told us in Your Word about the wise men. We don't know much about them, but we know why they were wise: they knew who Jesus was and came to worship Him.

I am glad that they were rich enough to bring such expensive gifts. I am glad the gifts came in time to protect the little family from greater hardship.

I would have had nothing to bring but myself. I can only give very little money or help in Your cause and You know why. But I love You and I want to love Jesus like the wise men did. Will *You* give me the gift of wisdom and love so that I may bring it to Jesus, Your Son? Will You also use Your gifts I bring and lay at the feet of Jesus to bring glory to Him? I ask for it in Jesus' name. Amen.

6
AT THE AGE OF TWELVE

The cruel and wicked Herod, the baby killer, died shortly after he had done that terrible deed. History tells us that he died in 4 B.C. That is the reason why Bible scholars put the birth of Christ at four to six years before the year 0. (B.C. means "before Christ." A.D. means *anno domini*, or "the year of the Lord," meaning after Christ. The year 0 divides B.C. and A.D.)

Herod died a fearful death. Tradition and historians tell us that he went mad. He succumbed to a mysterious disease marked by dementia and insatiable hunger.

After Herod's death an angel permitted Joseph and his family to return to Israel. Like any true Jew, Joseph and his wife must have been terribly homesick for their homeland. Jews love Jerusalem like a bridegroom loves his bride and they mourn and pine when they are not able to worship in that city.

Joseph wanted to return to Bethlehem. Was it because he saw Jesus in line of reign and as the heir to David's throne? But Archelaus, the son of Herod, reigned in Judea and he was, as history tells us, similar to his father in character.

Galilee was ruled by another son of Herod named Herod Antipas who was not so vicious. God guided the earthly parents of His Son to this area that was comparatively safe. The family settled in their former home in Nazareth.

We do not hear too much about the years of Jesus' childhood in Nazareth until He is twelve years old. We are told that Jesus went with His parents to the Temple at the age of twelve. Had He gone to the Temple before that it would have been of no significance since boys before that age had to sit with their mothers and sisters in the women's court.

We can be very sure that the boy Jesus worshiped every week in the synagogue in Nazareth, where again He sat with His mother while Joseph sat or stood in the men's area.

We have no Bible records of any formal education for Jesus. Historic research tells us that the Jewish woman of the house was responsible for the training of the children. Most men and women could read and whenever old or damaged scrolls were re-written by the scribes of a synagogue, people were permitted to take the old scrolls home. Scripture scrolls could never be burned or destroyed, only stored away or buried. It is safe to assume that God saw to it that His Son was taught just the *right* portions of the Scriptures and He provided the Old Testament scrolls, though the family was very poor.

Every Jewish boy had to memorize the entire book of Deuteronomy and some other Scripture portions. There were schools for children in the various villages, but we do not know if Jesus attended any. The poor very often could not afford to pay the scribe.

We know from Jewish history that a very famous rabbi named Hillel lived while Jesus was a boy. He is buried in the hills of Galilee. The profound influence of his teaching can even be found in some of Christ's sayings. One wonders, did the boy Jesus sit and listen to his teaching?

The child Jesus "grew, and waxed strong in spirit, filled with wisdom: and the grace of God was upon Him" (Luke 2:40). What those words truly mean can only be imagined when we know that Nazareth had the reputation of being a bad place (John 1:46)! The boy grew up surrounded by wickedness and temptation. Maybe He was teased for being a "goody-goody." Maybe He was also reminded by rude playmates that He was born out of wedlock. That fact must have been known though it is only suggested in a few simple verses in Luke 2:42-45. The full meaning can only be understood if we know the Jewish customs of that day.

The twelfth birthday marked a Jewish child's change from childhood to the "coming of age" as a youth. Girls got betrothed after that. Boys became young men with the right to inherit. However, the male child underwent a special training period and solemn ceremony at the age of thirteen. To become established as his father's son and into manhood, he came with his parents to the Temple at the age of twelve. And he stayed at the Temple school for several months of religious instruction while his parents went back home. At the end of his schooling a special ceremony took place. The Jews called it an adoption ceremony. The father took his son to the Temple and walked with him through the Court of the Gentiles, up the steps through the Beautiful Gate into the Court of the Women. After they crossed that court they walked up some more steps through another gate into the Court of the Men. The boy had never been there before. The father laid a prayer shawl around his son's shoulders and tied the little leather boxes, which contained portions of the Scriptures, on his son's forehead and right arm. He put one of the Torah scrolls in his son's arms and together they walked through the court to the steps of the Temple. Father and son turned and faced the people. The father put his hand on the boy's shoulder and announced: "This is my son. Today I give him *my* name!"

From that moment on a young man would be known

as James the son of Zebedee (Mark 1:19), or as Simon Bar-jonah (Matthew 16:17). (Bar means "son of." In modern times the Jews use "ben" instead of "bar," as in David Ben-Gurion.) Not until a young man went through that ceremony could he inherit his father's possessions, get married, pray for himself, read the Scriptures publicly or use his father's name.

There is no doubt that Joseph and Mary brought their firstborn son to the Temple on His twelfth birthday for such a purpose. Why they dared to do so, we don't know. The Bible doesn't say since it does not give us the details of Christ's first great humiliation.

When a boy entered the Temple school he was asked these questions: Are there Jewish women in your family for five generations? (It is the woman who carries the race in the Jewish culture; the man carries the inheritance.) When were you born and when was your parents' wedding feast?

Jesus had five generations of Jewish women, for Mary came from the line of David. There were two Gentile women in His lineage and one of these was Ruth (see Matthew 1:5), and her son became Jewish through another special adoption ceremony by Naomi. (We shall look into that story later.) So Jesus passed the first test!

The next question brought an answer that raised eyebrows. The parents had no wedding feast; Mary had been pregnant ahead of time! No illegitimate male was allowed to enter the Temple school. Didn't Joseph and Mary know that? Why did they try then? Did they hope that the scribes would believe the miracle of His birth? Joseph and Mary knew that it was the truth!

Jesus was never permitted to enter the Temple school. But He had so many questions! As His maturing mind began to grasp the concepts and symbols of the Temple rite, a new thought began to form in His mind. He knew that the Jews interpreted the Old Testament in such a way that every Scripture which foretold triumph, delivery and earthly greatness was applied to the Messiah. Every text which spoke of suffering, humility, shame and death was applied to the nation of Israel. The deliverer would come and save that downtrodden, humiliated nation and lead the people to new honor and glory.

Jesus watched the slaying of the Passover lamb and wondered, *who* was the lamb?

We don't know when the Holy Spirit put the new truth in His young forming mind that *He* was the Lamb! God Himself must have shown it to the young man at the edge of adulthood. Nobody else even thought of it, not even Mary, His mother.

Jesus knew that He wouldn't be allowed to stay at the Temple school. He knew there would never be an adoption ceremony and He would never become Jesus, the son of Joseph. He also knew that He had a right to be in that Temple school, so He walked in and sat down. He listened and asked questions. The learned doctors and scribes became intrigued by His bright mind and His brilliant answers. They forgot that He wasn't supposed to be there. He astonished them (Luke 2:47).

When His parents came back after three days, Jesus had things well under control. Whatever boggled His mind had been fully cleared up. He knew *who* He was and what He was doing. For the first time, in all due respect, He set His mother straight. "Don't you know that I was about My *Father's* business" (Luke 2:49)?

Nobody understood. But it didn't matter. Jesus did! Obediently He left the school and went back with His earthly parents while the rest of the boys of His age stayed. It meant embarrassment, disgrace and gossip. Everyone in Nazareth would now know that He was of no repute (Philippians 2:7). The young man, Jesus, came back and was subject to His parents (Luke 2:51).

What a lesson to the young people of today. What a

spirit of humility and trust in His heavenly Father! No wonder the Bible says that "Jesus increased in wisdom and stature, and in favor with God and man" (Luke 2:52).

God and people couldn't help but love Him! It's still the same. How can we know His life and not love Him?

LET'S PRAY: Dear Father, it must have been hard for You to see Your Son so humiliated at such a tender age. You suffered with Him and You stood by for You could see the end from the beginning long before the young boy Jesus did. I am still very young, too, and so often I don't understand why so many things have to happen. Life seems often unfair to me, and to others. Help me to trust You and be about Your business. Father, teach me now to subject myself willingly under anything which is ordained by You. For Jesus' example and sake. Amen.

7
YEARS OF PREPARATION

The Bible records nothing more about Christ for the next eighteen years of His life. Sometimes the silence of God's Word tells us as much as the written word.

At the end of that period we find Jesus beginning His life work. Joseph is not mentioned in Jesus' ministry, only Jesus' mother and brothers and sisters. It seems that Joseph must have died before Christ began His public ministry. This would have left Jesus to be Mary's provider. He was her firstborn Son (Luke 2:7)!

We also know that Jesus never married and obviously never inherited Joseph's possessions. We wonder if there was anything left behind by the carpenter father. The Bible does not tell us how Jesus made His livelihood until the age of thirty, but common tradition has it that the sons followed their father's trade.

Wood was and still is scarce in the Middle East. The houses of the common people were furnished with pillows, mats and stone. Even the dining table was often a flat stone. Only the rich could afford wooden articles and furniture. Nazareth did not boast of many rich inhabitants. It was too insignificant a city and was not on the main trade route or ever mentioned in any way, except in connection with the life of Jesus.

No doubt Christ's life was one of hard toil, poverty and long hours of manual labor. We don't know if His brothers or sisters were younger or older than He was. It depends much on whether Joseph was an elderly widower or a young man when he married Mary. If the brothers were older, Jesus had to be subject to them. If He was the firstborn, He bore the responsibility for the whole family.

No man under thirty years of age could ever teach, hold a religious office or lead out politically. People would simply not pay attention to such a person. Jesus therefore began His ministry when He was thirty years of age (Luke 3:23).

John the Baptist began preaching shortly before Jesus did. The forerunner of Christ was six months older. He had been living in the desert. It is possible that Zacharias and Elizabeth had died while the boy was of young age. Perhaps the sect of Essenes had taken him in and trained him for his work.

The Essenes were the most conservative and strict group of the three leading groups among the Jews. They lived in the desert near the Dead Sea in a hot dusty wilderness. They had renounced any contact with the rest of the Jews and considered Jerusalem too full of graft and wickedness to worship there. They did not sacrifice any longer but had a ritual cleansing bath. John perhaps adapted this bath into the rite of water baptism as he preached in the desert and the people came to hear him.

The Essenes lived only on desert products and dressed very simply. John lived on locusts and wild honey (Mark 1:6). (Locusts are not grasshoppers but pods from a carob tree.) He dressed in a camel's hair coat with a leather belt.

The Essenes had a great burden for the preservation of the Old Testament. A room was set aside in their community which they called the "scriptorium." There the men gathered to copy the scrolls of the Holy Word. (The famous Dead Sea Scrolls were found in caves near the Essene community.)

If the Essenes were the most conservative group of Christ's time— right-wingers we would call them today —the Sadducees would have to be put in the middle and the Pharisees to the left. The Sadducees were the aristocrats of society and were only a small group. They lived by the written Torah only and believed nothing that was not written. Since the Law of Moses does not talk about resurrection, they didn't even believe in life after death (Luke 20:27).

The Pharisees represented the common people and were a much larger group. They not only believed in the written Torah but made great demands on everybody by imposing the "oral Torah." These were unwritten interpretations and directions telling how to keep the Mosaic Laws. The Pharisees measured their holiness by the amount of ceremonies they kept. And they had many hundreds of ordinances, rituals and legalistic interpretations which made life burdensome and the religious experience a fearful misery for the common people.

The Temple ceremonies and the daily sacrifice had become a meaningless, dead ritual. The priests and the masses had forgotten why a lamb was slain and why the yearly festivals were held. The three main festivals were Passover, the Feast of Weeks (Pentecost), and the Feast of Tabernacles (Numbers 28:16-31; Leviticus 23:33-36). Every respectable Jew was expected to go to Jerusalem to celebrate these feasts.

The Day of Atonement (described in Leviticus 16), Israel's most important day of the year in Moses' time, was not kept any longer according to the Old Testament Law. It had not been observed for the last four hundred years since the Jews came back from Babylonian captivity and the Ark of the Covenant had been lost. There is no atonement without a mercy seat for the priest had no place to bring the blood without the Ark (Leviticus 16:14,15).

Though the Jews had a magnificent Temple (built by Herod), the Holy of Holies was an empty room which nobody ever entered. No wonder the people had to depend on their good works and the rigid keeping of every written and unwritten law, for they had no place of mercy to come to.

The Sanhedrin Council, or often called the Great Council, ruled the Jewish people. Though the Romans had the upper hand when it came to taxes and keeping revolts down, they didn't interfere too much with the national and religious life of the Jews. The official language in Israel was Greek and not Hebrew. Greek was spoken all over the Roman empire. The Hebrew language was only used in the Jewish worship services in the Temple and the synagogues. It was considered a sacred language and any praying had to be done in Hebrew.

The language of the peasants was Aramaic which was a simplified Greek mixed with Hebrew colloquialisms. It was not a very precise language. All official communication or writing was done in Greek. When the ruling council met, they conducted their meetings in the Greek language.

The Sanhedrin consisted of thirty-five Sadducees and thirty-five Pharisees. It was a religious assembly. The high priest presided over them. Whenever issues were decided and the Sadducees agreed and the Pharisees opposed unitedly, it was the high priest who broke the tie. By this authority he became the most powerful figure in the country.

Once the Israelites had had an anointed priesthood called by God (Exodus 30:30). When the Jews returned from Babylon they had no records left. They could not tell who had come from the family of Aaron and Zadok (Ezekiel 48:11,12; Ezra 2:62,63). The Gentiles had deliberately destroyed the genealogy of the priesthood.

People still knew pretty well from which tribe they came, but family records were harder to come by and the high priest had to be appointed.

The appointed priesthood had degenerated over the centuries to the place that in Christ's time the high priest was appointed by Rome. The emperor gave the leadership every year to the man who offered him the most money, for money was Rome's highest priority.

Fraud, bribery, even murder were often used to gain that position and no spiritual significance or true worship could be found in connection with it anymore. The priesthood was a matter of money, not of serving God, in most areas of the national life. Corruption reigned! One stole from the other. The high priest bought himself into a position. Then he sold the positions under him to the highest bidder. He sent tax farmers out to the people to collect the taxes for Rome. They paid him and also feathered their own nest.

The tax farmers sold positions to the publicans who sat in the places of traffic and collected taxes for anything imaginable. The common people bore the final burden. The people hated and despised all tax collectors but could do nothing but grit their teeth and bear the oppression. The Romans had no mercy when it came to revolts and outbreaks of violence and discontent. They crucified anyone, slaves and foreigners, who showed the slightest sign of rebellion to Rome. The Jews had long gotten used to the sight of crosses where anyone connected with any political or religious upheaval had to die a slow and agonizing death. Roman citizens never died that way. The Romans saved that cruel death for slaves and foreigners only.

Into that atmosphere of greed, violence, distrust and spiritual apathy came a voice. It was a voice that came from the desert, the wilderness, and it was the voice of John the Baptist. "Repent," he said, "repent and get ready, for the kingdom of God is at hand" (Matthew 3:1,2).

LET'S PRAY: Dear Father in heaven, I never knew into what impossible circumstances You sent Your Son to save us all! How Your Father's heart must have ached when You watched Your chosen people be so misled. Father, protect Your children of today from legalism and empty form and rigid rituals as a means of atonement. Help us to remember that such things don't count with You. Your kingdom is built on true repentance and love and we come to You through Christ. Amen.

8
THIS IS MY BELOVED SON

John's message was not a message of salvation; it was a call to clean up the corruption of individual lives and the affairs of the nation. The words of John stabbed and shook the people; he was neither gentle nor flattering to them. He pointed without fear to the sins of his time and denounced the scribes and Pharisees, even when they came to him for baptism as a sign of their repentance. He called them vipers (Luke 3:7)!

The common people were weary and without hope. They could not find comfort and peace anywhere, neither in their religious practices nor in their daily life. They had lost connection with the living God and Satan tortured them with guilt and fear. Because they had no place to go for forgiveness and mercy, John's preaching brought deep conviction of their sins.

"What shall we do then?" (Luke 3:10), they asked.

"Be kind to each other," he said, "share, beware of injustice and violence" (Luke 3:11-14)!

It's obvious that John did not understand fully the mission of the Messiah whose way he came to prepare (Matthew 11:2,3; Mark 1:2,3). He most likely looked for Him as the one who would deliver Israel from political oppression and believed that the people had to make things right with God first before it could happen. No doubt the prophecies which were given at his birth, that

Israel would be delivered out of the hand of their enemies (Luke 1:68-74), encouraged such thinking.

Multitudes of people came to John wondering and hoping: Was he the Christ (Luke 3:15)? *Christ* is the Greek word for the Hebrew word, *messiah*, which means, "the anointed one." John discouraged such thinking and told the masses that someone greater than he was to come who would baptize with fire and the Holy Spirit (Luke 3:16).

Just as we don't know how Christ left His heavenly home so we don't have any details about His departure from His earthly home in Nazareth. If He was the head of the house, He knew that Mary depended on Him for a livelihood. If He was under the authority of older brothers, He might have left under their protest. The Bible indicates that His brothers and sisters didn't believe in His divine calling (John 7:5). But when the hour came, nobody could stop Jesus Christ!

After all the years of obscurity, living as a peasant and giving no indications that He had come to this earth for a special mission, Jesus set out for the Judean desert. In the eyes of His people He was nobody. He came from Galilee. The Judeans looked down on Galileans. He had no money, no fame, no influence, no friends, no political strings to pull. He had no formal education, not even Temple school. He didn't even have a family name. Joseph never adopted him. He wasn't married. He wasn't known for any act of bravery or rebellion against the Romans.

A young man in the clothing of a Galilean peasant walked up to John and asked for baptism. John and Jesus were cousins, but they had obviously never met. If John had grown up with the Essenes, it would be reasonable to believe that his seclusion kept him from visiting *any* relatives. The Essenes had absolutely nothing to do with the rest of the nation. Even when John began to preach he never set foot in Jerusalem or any other city. He stayed in the desert and the people had to seek him out to hear him (Matthew 3:1,5,6).

Jesus, on the other hand, had grown up in the remote hills of Galilee and people didn't travel for fun and family visits often. Life was too hard for that. It was a burden enough to travel three times a year to Jerusalem to fulfill the obligation of attending the main religious festivals.

We do not know how John knew immediately who Christ was. No doubt, he had been told in his childhood about the miraculous birth and happenings of his cousin, Jesus. (Legend tells us that John's father, Zacharias, was killed by Herod's soldiers for refusing to disclose the hiding place of the baby Jesus.) When Jesus asked John to baptize Him, the Baptist shrunk back and said, "You need to baptize me" (Matthew 3:14).

Jesus shook His head. He didn't argue with His preacher cousin that He indeed was the higher in rank and had a right to baptize any preacher. He simply said: "I must do it to submit Myself to the lot of humanity and set the right example" (Matthew 3:15).

John did as the Lord told him to do.

When Jesus came out of the murky Jordan water something beautiful happened. One wonders if Jesus was bowed in prayer when it happened or if His face was lifted up to heaven in holy communion with His Father. No doubt about it, Jesus Christ already knew how to pray. In His long years of quiet preparation He had been taught and prepared by the heavenly Father and the Holy Spirit for His coming ministry. Jesus knew what was ahead of Him. He knew who the Lamb was, though nobody else did! He knew He was facing an impossible task as a human being. He had chosen to face His commission as a human *only*, with no extra heavenly privileges or divinity mixed into it (Philippians 2:5-8).

While the masses are milling around and John watches the lone figure walk out of the water, the heavens open. Whenever God's heaven opens, bright light pours out, for God *is* light (1 John 1:5).

A voice, God's voice, is heard and He says, "This *is* My beloved Son, in whom I am well pleased" (Matthew 3:17).

What is happening? God Himself is conducting an adoption ceremony for His only precious Son. He knows that Joseph never adopted Jesus, that He was only "supposed" to be Joseph's son (Luke 3:23). To set the record straight for His chosen people's tradition, Jesus not only lets Himself be baptized like a sinner but His Father adopts Him according to Jewish custom.

And God does more than that! Jewish kings and priests were anointed with oil upon their heads. The oil was a *symbol* of the Holy Spirit which hopefully would direct the steps of an anointed man. God didn't anoint Jesus with oil; He did more for Him! Instead of a symbol, He sent the real substance to His Son at that special ceremony. The Holy Spirit came down like a dove and rested on the Saviour's head. And He remained with Jesus (John 1:32)!

John was overwhelmed. He had been told by God's Spirit that he would see a special sign on the one who *was* the Son of God. Now he witnessed it (John 1:33, 34).

Shaken to the core, in a flash of divine insight, in deep reverence and humility John stretched out his hand and pointed at the figure bathed in God's light: "Behold," he said, "the Lamb of God, which taketh away the sin of the world" (John 1:29).

LET'S PRAY: Dear Jesus, when I was baptized I knew why! I had so many sins that needed to be buried and put away. You had no sin, but for my sake You became like a sinner. For my sake You set an example! What can I say but "thank You, and I love You." I rejoice greatly that the heavenly Father adopted You as a human Son, Jesus, for by doing so He adopted me too! It's almost too hard to comprehend it all, but I know that I don't need to understand it to receive it. All I need to do is accept it in Your name. Amen.

9
SATAN TRIES!

That John the Baptist did not fully understand what he was saying when he called Jesus "the Lamb of God" is evident at a later time when we find him in prison. He began to doubt Christ's calling and sent Him a message (Matthew 11:2,3). As we read the Bible words we cannot help but wonder if John's unspoken message in his question was: "Aren't You going to *deliver* me out of this dungeon, *if* You *are* the Deliverer of Israel?"

Jesus didn't deliver John from prison and death (Matthew 14:10). He didn't very often do the humanly predictable thing.

One would think, from the human standpoint, that Christ should have begun His ministry right after His baptism when people watched the display of His heavenly glory. What better time could there have been to impress the people and start off "right"?

Christ never acted according to human reasoning, scheme or tactic but let Himself be led by the Holy Spirit alone. And the Spirit led Him into the wilderness (Matthew 4:1). Jesus walked away from the crowds into the quiet desert to commune with His Father. Was He led there because it was the only place He could be alone and undisturbed? Or did He have to go there because He had to meet His archenemy on his own "demon-stration" ground?

The Bible tells us several times that demons wander in desert places (Isaiah 13:21; Matthew 12:43; Luke 8:29; 11:24). The desert is a convincing example to the human life of what happens when the life-giving element of water is missing. (Water is a symbol of the Holy Spirit, John 7:38,39.)

Jesus stayed in the wilderness for forty days. He had no food to eat (Matthew 4:2). Anyone who ever visited the Judean desert will tell you that *nothing* lives or grows there. It's a desolate area of many rocks, dried-up, thorny fruitless bushes and no other shelter but the shade of harsh big boulders. At some times of the year little rivulets of water appear, and Jesus must have found some water to quench His thirst. A human body can survive a forty-day fast, but only a few days without water. Christ had come to live under the human laws of survival and never used superhuman means to exist while He was on earth. So the Bible tells us that He had no *food* for forty days (Luke 4:2). In the Jewish way of thinking the number forty stands for one generation. Whenever the number forty is used, it indicates the length of human endurance (Numbers 14:33; Deuteronomy 2:7; 1 Kings 19:8; Acts 7:23,30,36).

At the end of forty days Christ's body felt weak from hunger. Satan knew that his moment had come. Now was the time to tempt the man Jesus. Satan and his demons do not only love to tempt through the avenues of the human body, but they also prefer to attack when the body is weakened by hunger, lack of proper rest, strain or sickness.

Christ's body was exhausted by lack of proper nourishment. We do not know how much He had slept either during the cold desert nights, without a bed and proper shelter.

The Bible does not tell us how the devil appeared to the Lord. Some Bible scholars suggest that the whole temptation was only a mind battle of strong ideas and thoughts Christ was assailed with. But the Word of God tells us that the tempter came to Him and spoke to Him (Luke 4:3).

Satan *is* a person, just as angels are individual beings or persons, too. It is a real possibility that the devil approached Jesus as an angel of light. This is his favorite disguise when he tries to deceive human beings (2 Corinthians 11:14).

Christ was human and used no supernatural gifts to detect, fight, or recognize Satan. Maybe He wondered if His Father had sent Him some extra help because He was so faint with hunger. However, Jesus *knew* that it wasn't God's angel when Satan said the first sentence. "If You are the Son of God . . . " (Luke 4:3).

The little word, "if " showed the true source of "help" Christ was to receive. God's angels had announced thirty years before that the Son of God was born. They sang with joy about it. They *knew* that Jesus was His Father's Son. They would have never questioned Him!

Satan is neither creative nor very original. He copies God in everything. He also uses the same tactics over and over when he tries to tempt and deceive. His favorite way to begin his approach is with a question. The kind of question that would put doubt into a person's mind! Satan knew well that Jesus was the Second Adam (1 Corinthians 15:45), and he tried to trip Him the same way he did our first parents (Genesis 3:2-5). He began his approach in the Garden of Eden with a question too (Genesis 3:1)!

With Christ, it seemed that Satan would have a much easier time. When he tempted Adam and Eve about food, they were neither hungry, tired nor exhausted. When he suggested that Christ should make bread out of stones, Jesus was starved. Maybe some stones actually looked like the flat oriental loaves which were eaten by the Jews of His day. Perhaps the evil visitor picked some of those stones up and tried to hand them to Jesus. What an overpowering temptation when a person is starved to the point of death!

Christ was at the end of human endurance, but He was ruled at all times by His spirit, not by the needs of the flesh. He used the *only* weapon and defense that is stronger than Satan's cunning devices: the Word of God.

Calmly He said, "It is written . . . " (Luke 4:4). Christ didn't debate or argue. He didn't analyze the suggestion, innocent and helpful as it appeared at first sight. He didn't point out to Satan that "if" He did as Satan suggested He would use His divinity to gratify His own needs in a way other humans wouldn't be able to. He would also break the natural laws of God—laws He Himself had laid when the earth was made! If He changed mineral into a grain, He would permit an inconsistancy which Satan would love to exploit later when evolution was taught on this globe.

No doubt Christ saw all of this and more but He didn't state it all. He gave the most important reason why He must reject the idea: Satan had his priorities mixed up. Bread was important to the human life but it wasn't life itself: God's Word is the life-giving source (Deuteronomy 8:4)!

Satan knew he had lost his first round!

He tried again and on a higher level. If God and His kingdom was so important to Jesus, why not tempt Him on that issue? Satan took the famished weary human form of Jesus up on a very high mountain and showed Him the kingdoms of the world. "If you bow down, you can have it all" he said (Matthew 4:9; Luke 4:7).

What was the evil one doing? He was trying several things: first he tried to establish his *right* to be the ruler of this world. After all, hadn't Adam sold out to him?

So, if Christ would acknowledge him as the rightful ruler of the world's kingdoms, nobody could dispute his right ever again.

Next, he offered Jesus a compromise. He could have the crown without the cross! Why not ask for glory without suffering, worldly honor and greatness without the path of rejection, betrayal and death?

Christ reacted less calmly the second time. He told Satan to get lost (Matthew 4:10). Jesus knew that He had come to dispute Satan's *right* to own the world. That was His mission, to take away Satan's claim of total ownership upon the whole human race.

"Only *One* deserves to be worshiped," Christ pointed out. He had established another priority (Matthew 4:10; Luke 4:8).

Satan was desperate. He tried once more. He took Jesus to Jerusalem, the beloved city of God. He stood with Him on the pinnacle of the Temple (Luke 4:9). The Temple shimmered below them; the crowds surged everywhere. Satan used the most deceptive temptation that he can ever use to tempt any human being: He quoted promises of God for the wrong motive (Luke 4:10; see also Psalm 91:11)!

Again, it sounded so "right," so innocent. It would even glorify God, wouldn't it? "Look," he said to Jesus, "if You claim God's promises and float down as one coming from above, the masses will accept You much easier as God's messenger. It will further Your and Your Father's cause."

Christ answered with *one* sentence: "Don't ever tempt God" (Luke 4:12; see also Deuteronomy 6:16)!

How can a person tempt God when claiming His promises? When a person puts his trust in the promises of God and tries to *force* God to honor those promises, he is always off center.

Christ didn't put His trust in bread or in His divine

calling or even in the promises of His Father. He had *all* His priorities straight. Christ put His full trust in God Himself. His top priority was the will of His Father. So He didn't need to put on a big show or try to glorify Himself. He could quietly trust His Father alone and not even tell Him *when* to use any of His promises. The Bible tells us that Christ was tempted in all ways as we are (Hebrews 4:15).

So, the three temptations Satan used on Christ, he will use most often on Christ's followers. He will sometimes mix up the order of the temptations and use whatever fits the occasion best. With Adam and Eve he used the lust of the eye first, then the appetite and next the promise to become wise and like God.

We must beware of Satan's deceptions. He will come as an angel of light to bring us great new insights. The only way to test whether the new "light" is from the Holy Spirit or Satan is to look for a word that shows doubt—"If you are the Son of God . . . " (Luke 4:9). Does the new "light" question the role of the Son of God or is He established more clearly as your *only* Saviour and Lord by it (Acts 4:12)? Anyone who sets out to put doubt about Jesus Christ into this world serves Satan and the anti-Christ (1 John 4:1-3).

Let's also beware of helping God out with our own human schemes and devices, even when we try to glorify Him. Whenever we try a shortcut to glory and avoid suffering at any cost, we are not doing it God's way.

God's promises *are* true, but who are we to tell Him when or how to use them? Maybe His wisdom sees fit to use a different promise than we have claimed at a given time or place. Maybe since our Father in heaven knows us so well, He tries to protect us from self-exaltation and a harsh fall when He doesn't come through in the way we demand of Him! To make us use God's promises in the wrong way is *still* Satan's most wily and powerful temptation and trick, even today. We must *never* look at God as our cosmic bellhop. Just because we claim a promise, we can never force God to act according to *our* prayer and will in fulfilling it! God will honor our faith—but faith with the wrong motive or assumption becomes presumption.

Christ knew all that and He answered accordingly—by quoting Scripture. He said, "Satan, get lost. I trust God alone. I don't need to plan My own life and mission. I don't need to put on a show for God's glory. All I need to do is to wait upon Him and He will take care of Me. I'd rather die on the spot of hunger and exhaustion than to ever *force* My Father to act after *My* will! He *will* come through when He sees best!"

Satan had to leave after that; he always will when he gets that answer. And God came through. Angels ministered to Jesus when the attack was over (Matthew 4:11). The Father knew that His human Son had spent His last ounce of strength—physically, emotionally, mentally and spiritually—and God will never permit anyone to be tempted beyond his endurance point (1 Corinthians 10: 13).

Jesus was tempted with much more force than we ever will be. He, as the second Adam, won the victory. Under devastating, overpowering handicaps which Adam did not have to face, Jesus proved that it *could* be done.

In Him we can win over *any* temptation at any place and time, if we are willing to do it *His* way!

LET'S PRAY: Dear Jesus, I don't know what it is like to be starved and go without food for a day or for a week. Even when I diet, I can eat a little when the hunger gets to me. It is beyond me how You endured it all, but I don't need to understand it. All I need to do is to keep my eyes on *You* and do as You did—even when temptations come into my life like a flood! I shall just say to Satan: "It is written" and quote the Bible text Your Holy Spirit will give me for that moment.

Help me never to use Your promises for selfish reasons. Teach me *how* to use them right. Protect me from the sin of self-exaltation and presumption and set my priorities straight, for Your name's sake. Amen.

10
FOLLOW ME

Strengthened by His heavenly visitors (Matthew 4:11) Jesus walked out of the wilderness into inhabited areas to begin His work. God's time at last had come; everything was ready for the Messiah. Everything? Everything and everybody who *wanted* to be ready, was ready.

God had done all He could. The prophecies pointed toward immediate fulfillment. Special happenings at the birth of John and Jesus had drawn the attention of the people to the nearness of the Messiah's coming. John, as the forerunner of Christ, had stirred up the whole nation with his message of repentance and expectancy.

John's work had reached such proportion that he drew the attention of the Jewish leaders to himself. They got so concerned about him that they began an investigation and sent delegates out to question him.

"I am not the Christ," John said humbly but fearlessly. "I am a voice in the wilderness—to make straight the way of the Lord" (John 1:19-23; Isaiah 40:3).

That meaningful prophecy in Isaiah which John quoted illustrated a very ancient but well-known custom. When a king or other high dignitary traveled across a land, a man or group of people had to be forerunners—go ahead of and make the way safe for the royal chariot. Chuck holes were filled with stones, uneven surfaces were leveled, landslides were removed, so that the king could move forward without delay or hindrance.

John saw himself as such a forerunner to Christ. And he knew *who* the Messiah was. While the haughty men from Jerusalem questioned him, he said: "There standeth one among you whom ye know not" (John 1:26).

Several times the Bible records moments when John the Baptist recognized Jesus among the people and every time he pointed Him out as the Lamb of God (John 1:29,30,36; 3:27-30). Jesus on the other hand made no obvious outward display or did anything to draw the attention of the crowds to Himself. He mingled as a peasant among the peasants. He listened and seemed in no hurry to make any claims.

John's powerful preaching drew people to Bethabara beyond Jordan. The place wasn't far from the spot where Jericho had fallen under the power of God. The people were excited to think that perhaps soon the great deliverer would come and overthrow the hated Romans as He had defeated the Canaanites in ancient times.

Once more John sees Jesus walking quietly among the people and again he points at Him and says, "Behold the Lamb of God" (John 1:36). Two of John's disciples listened. It was a custom of that time for famous leaders, rabbis or teachers to gather around themselves a group of pupils or disciples who wanted to learn and study. John had obviously acquired enough status and fame so that a group of steady followers traveled with him and were taught by him.

Two of his disciples, John and Andrew, heard the words of the Baptist and wondered. What does he mean: the Lamb of God? They followed the stranger. He didn't look like a Messiah, at least not the way they had pictured Him. He wore a simple Galilean garment and was haggared, like one who hadn't eaten well for awhile. Who was He?

Jesus turned quietly and asked, "What seek ye?"

In answer the two men asked, "Rabbi [Teacher], where do you live?"

The two disciples had too many questions to answer in a wayside discussion. So Jesus invited them to the place where He was staying. It had to be the home of a friend, for He had no other home (John 1:39).

Whatever was said between Christ and the two young men convinced them to the point where they went out to find more disciples for the Master. Andrew found his brother Simon. "We have found the Messiah," he rejoiced. Simon did not need a second invitation; he came along immediately.

Jesus looked at him, "You are Simon, the son of John, but I am giving you another name." (John 1:42)!

In the Jewish culture a name is more than a name. It's almost impossible to comprehend in our modern thinking what significance a personal Jewish name carried. It represented the essence of its bearer and very often people received new names or changed their names as their mode of living changed. The Talmud tells us that the name given to a person affected his future, his personality, and his life! God Himself changed names in the Old Testament (Genesis 17:5,15; 32:28). He Himself picked the human name for His Son (Matthew 1:21).

Now at the beginning of His ministry Jesus took upon Himself the authority to change a person's name—and with it his life! Simon is the Hebrew name that means "hearing." Christ said, "You shall be called a stone [*Cephas*]" (John 1:42). The Roman name for Cephas is *Petros* or Peter.

As we find out later, Simon bar-Jona wasn't much of a hearer. He was an impulsive talker and a hothead. It took quite a while before he became a stone or rock who couldn't be moved. But Christ knew that he had a sincere heart and was eager to serve. So He showed His faith in Peter's ability to grow and mature into solidness by giving him a future name.

Christ Himself went into Galilee to find Philip. When

He saw him, He said, "Follow Me." This is the first record of a man who was called by Christ taking the initiative. Who was Philip that Christ would go to the special effort to find and call him? Our human thinking would assume that he had to be someone of outstanding talent and importance. He had to be influential so he could help the new ministry along, since Jesus Himself had no special earthly strings to pull.

The only one who tells us about Philip is John. Bible commentators say that most likely John, Philip, Peter and James came from the same place (John 1:44). Let's first notice that nobody bothered to tell Philip about the Messiah. Jesus Himself had to call him. Philip obviously was neither outstanding nor important enough for anyone to send him to the Messiah. He didn't become a famous figure after he was called into discipleship either.

We know three things about Philip: he wanted to share Jesus with others; he was careful to do right and be obedient to authority; he was eager to learn and gain better insight.

The first time we hear of Philip we find that he began to share Jesus the moment he found and followed Him (John 1:45). The next time we read about Philip was when the Greeks came to him in the Temple and wanted to see Jesus. Philip did not take the initiative but went to talk to Andrew (John 12:21,22). One wonders if he was troubled because Gentiles wanted to be with the Lord. Was it right? Philip didn't want to break any traditional rules unless the Lord said so!

The third time Philip is mentioned was when, in the upper room, he posed a question, "Lord, show us the Father, and we shall be satisfied" (John 14:8, *RSV*). The fact that Philip made the statement doesn't mean that he was dull or less intelligent than the rest. Perhaps all the disciples wondered about the same thing, but nobody wanted to expose his ignorance. Philip was so eager to understand that he dared to ask (John 14:8-11).

So, who was this man who heard the first "follow Me" from Jesus Christ? He was an average man whose occupation was so insignificant that the Bible doesn't even tell us how he made a living. He had neither wealth nor special talent. All he had were those three beautiful traits!

With His first call to follow Him, Christ set us a pattern and example: *any* person who is willing to share, obey and learn may become His disciple. Christ does not ask first for ability but for ready availability.

We do not know what happened to Christ's other disciples who came to Him before Philip, but suddenly we find them back in their fishing boats (Matthew 4:18).

Jesus finds them and calls them to a new life work: "Follow Me, I'll make you fishers of men" (Matthew 4:19). We do not know if they had second thoughts after they first met Him or if the group ran out of food and money after a while and had to resume their professions. We do know that when Jesus did call them, they left everything behind and followed Him immediately (Matthew 4:20).

As we look through the New Testament we find that Jesus ended up with twelve disciples (Mark 3:14-19). Eleven of them came from the northern part of Israel (Galilee), the area the southern Jews looked down upon! Only one came from the respected south—Judas Iscariot! We have no record how he joined the group. It says nowhere that Christ called him. He most likely jumped on the bandwagon when things began to look up and Christ's fame began to spread. After all, one never knew but what there could be a good position waiting after Christ gained leadership and power—so let's hang around and see. Was this what Judas thought?

Not everyone who was called by Christ to follow Him

obeyed the call. One of the most tragic tales of the Gospels is the story of the rich young ruler (Mark 10:17-22).

He came to Jesus with a respectful sensible question. He came to the *right* person and asked *right* things. He didn't expect the kind of answer he got. It wasn't the *right* answer for him. One wonders if he ever heard Jesus say: "Come, follow *Me*"?

Maybe he listened only as far as the point where Jesus asked him to sell all that he had. The rich young man walked away—sorrowful! What did he do after he left Jesus? No doubt he continued to keep all the laws and rules of his time and remained a respected, wealthy citizen. Maybe the common people looked up to him. Maybe he even taught religion as a Pharisee and a member of the Sanhedrin!

But as far as we know he never followed Jesus. And all his riches, law-keeping and honorable deeds never gained for him what Jesus had to offer—entrance into God's kingdom (Mark 10:21).

LET'S PRAY: Dear Jesus, I want to follow You! I am nobody, just like Philip, but I can do what he did: I can tell others to come see you. I can also work together with others and help those who lead out.

Give me a searching mind and a willing heart, dear Lord, and help me to listen to *all* You have to say, not only part of it.

May I never trust money or the "keeping and doing of the right things" as a means to earn heaven. May I keep my eyes on You alone and follow You wherever You lead— right into the kingdom and the glory forever. Amen.

11
TOWARD HUMAN DIGNITY

Many people picture Jesus Christ as a person who portrayed only humble and quiet non-resistance. They think of Him as a soft and almost feminine character who showed none of the traits attributed to the masculine personality of His or our time.

Nothing could be further from the truth. Jesus displayed in all His actions a courage which can only be fully seen if we get ourselves acquainted with the prevailing attitudes of His time. Who, but someone who was not afraid of anything or anybody, would have *dared* to call Matthew, the publican, as His disciple (Matthew 9:9)? It was one thing to call humble fishermen and "Mister Nobody" as His close associates. After all, He simply had no access to educated, rich people and had no choice but to call peasants to follow Him. But *why* would He stir up a hornet's nest by calling a despised and hated tax-gatherer to join His group?

The Jews hated no one more than those who worked with and for the Romans. They had no association with anyone who "betrayed" his Jewish heritage and cultural loyalties. And the tax collectors were doubly hated. They not only worked with the national enemy they also enriched themselves at the expense of their own people. Why then would Jesus arouse great prejudice among the Jewish leaders and even perplex His own disciples by calling such a despised man? Because Christ *never* looked at the outside of anything or anybody, ever! He always looked at the heart. He still does! And Matthew's heart wanted to follow Jesus, but he would have never dared to offer himself. He knew that he was a national outcast, a reject, a no-good in the eyes of his society.

Christ walked toward Matthew's tax booth when He and His disciples visited Capernaum on the shores of the Sea of Galilee. "Follow Me," He said to the astonished publican, and Matthew got up and followed Him. When he left *all*, he did just that.

He did more than that: he gave a great feast in Christ's honor. After all, he had acquired enough wealth as a Roman tax farmer that he could afford to give big dinners. He invited all his friends to the festivities, and the only friends he had were other publicans and the outcasts of society. No respectable Jew would ever step under his roof. But Jesus did! No doubt, Matthew had Him sit in the seat of honor, which was at the right side of the host.

The Jewish leaders were furious. In order to effectively make their point, they did not go to Jesus but they approached His disciples. If they could upset and disturb His disciples, they could hurt Jesus twice as much. They liked to do this and they tried hard to cause disharmony and misunderstandings among Christ's followers.

Christ looked at the hearts of these leaders and He answered them personally. "You don't think you need Me," He said. "You see yourselves whole and well and perfect. Why won't you at least let me help those who *know* they are in need of My healing power and love? What am I taking away from you if I am kind and give My attention to them? They are people who have feelings, hearts that long for love and acceptance and I came to this earth to bring help to *anyone* who wants it" (Matthew 9:12,13; 11:28-30).

Neither Matthew nor the disciples thought or even

dreamed, at that controversial meal, that some day in the future the rejected sinner and publican Matthew would write one of the Gospels of the New Testament. As was typical of Christ's way of doing things, He loved to make those who came last in the eyes of the world first in His kingdom. Jesus loved people and the common people must have loved Him and liked to be with Him.

Was it because He made them feel accepted? Did He treat even the lowest and poorest with a respect and love which gave them a new sense of human dignity, a sense of self worth and importance?

When Christ got ready to perform His first miracle, He didn't go before the Jewish leaders or the Sanhedrin to impress them. It happened again among those who were seeking His presence and company (John 2:1-11).

Someone invited Jesus and His disciples to a wedding feast in Cana, a little village up in the hills of Galilee. The place wasn't far from Nazareth where He grew up. It must not have been a well-to-do home where the party was given, for the bridegroom ran out of wine before it was time to send the guests home.

We know that a wedding celebration took at least seven days and it takes a lot of food and drink to entertain a house full of people for a whole week. It was of utmost embarrassment to a home to run out of wine at such an occasion. Wine, to the Jewish people since Old Testament times, was a symbol of joy. To run out of it had to be a bad sign for the beginning of a new home.

Mary, the mother of Jesus, was present too. It seems she might even have been one of the relatives who was in charge of the meals. "They are out of wine," she said to Jesus.

"Woman," He said, "My hour is not yet come!"

Was Christ rude to His mother? No, He was not! The form He used to address her when He called her "woman" was a sign of great respect and adoration. Today we would use the form "madam," or "honored lady" if we wanted to express similar sentiments.

Christ always honored His parents to set the right example for us. But He never let anyone, not even His mother, interfere with His divine mission. Mary should have remembered. He set her straight the first time at the age of twelve when she scolded Him in the Temple. "Must I not be about My Father's business?" He asked her kindly.

Now He reminds her that her motherly ties and ambitions cannot push or coax Him. Mary dreams the same dream everyone else does: Jesus Christ has come to deliver Israel from political oppression. The sooner He "proves" Himself to everyone the faster they all will follow Him when He calls for a revolution.

But Jesus Christ could wait—until *God* told Him what to do and when.

Mary might have been impatient and eager for her Son not only to justify Himself, but her too. People had never completely forgotten about the questionable time element in Jesus' birth. Not only Jesus, but also His mother had carried a stain on their reputations ever since. Wasn't it time to "prove" that He was of divine origin? Mary *knew* it was true; wasn't it time to let others be convinced, too? Most people just snickered about the story of a virgin birth. (They still do!)

"Mother, I shall not do *any* thing unless it is in God's plan and time," the Son said to her.

She had lived with Him for thirty years. She knew He hadn't closed the door to her request completely. She trusted Him. She *knew* better than anyone else that He was God's Son. She gave clear orders. "Whatever He says, do it." And Jesus honored her faith (John 2:5).

When He changed the water in the six waterpots to wine, He produced at least seventy gallons of quality wine. The servants didn't tell anyone where the wine came from until it had been tasted (John 2:9).

Why were they hesitating to tell? The wine was served from vessels of water which the people used for foot-washing. The vessels of drinking water were much smaller, the size that a woman could carry from the well to her house. Every house had several kinds of water pots. Vessels of honor (the fresh drinking water), vessels of dishonor (the water for washing and other household use), vessels of wrath (garbage stuff) (2 Timothy 2:20, 21; Romans 9:21-23).

The servants filled the vessels of dishonor with fresh water. Christ then changed the water into a symbol of joy and special blessing of God (Psalm 104:15).

Jesus never did anything by accident or on the spur of the moment. Everything He ever said or did had a deep meaning and a clear purpose. When He put delicious new wine into the water pots, He didn't do it so that later generations of His followers could argue whether He had changed water into grape juice or fermented wine. That is not the issue at all. It's not even debatable that the Jewish people have always used wine as part of their meals and worship—from ancient times on. It is an established fact and the Bible does not condemn wine but the over-indulgence and misuse of it (Ephesians 5:18; Proverbs 20:1).

When Jesus performed His first miracle, He did it, according to the Bible, to strengthen the faith of His disciples (John 2:11). They would need that new belief in Him to withstand the unbelief and prejudice of the Jewish leaders in days to come.

No doubt, Jesus also wanted to honor His mother's complete trust in Him and bring a special gift to the newlyweds. He honored a poor home not only with His presence but with something only the rich could usually afford. And He gave it to them with a symbolic message that said, "Don't worry about the outer form of a water pot or how a person appears to others. Let Me touch what's inside. I can take the most humble element and change it into something beautiful and new, if you trust Me.

"I do not expect My followers to run around with a sour face and in fasting and ashes all their lives. There is a time for joy and festivities in the human life too."

Christ, with His presence, not only honored the institution of wedding celebrations and marriages, He also let it be known that happy social activities have a place in His followers' lives. Since He is our example in all things, let us approach life as He did. He avoided any extremes and we should too!

What a thoughtful, considerate and kind man Jesus must have been. No wonder the people loved to be with Him. Isn't it time we as His followers act more like Him? (See Proverbs 18:24 *KJV*.)

LET'S PRAY: Dear Jesus, I need to contemplate Your life a lot more than I do, for by my beholding I become changed into Your image. I want to be more like You but I have a long way to go yet! People are not as eager to have me around as they were You. I know why. I am not always friendly, thoughtful and unselfish, and I try to have my own way. I pout and my bad moods often destroy other people's good times.

Jesus, take the bitter waters of my soul and make them into Your new wine. Make me a wellspring of joy to a sad world. Let me remember that the outer form of politeness doesn't count. Remove my phony front; change and fill me—with You! In Your name, I dare ask for the impossible in my joyless life. Amen.

12
A CHANCE TO BELIEVE

The first miracle Jesus did was for the benefit of His disciples, His family and some personal friends. The story of it might have been told among some peasants in Galilee but it surely didn't make headline news in the nation of Israel. Newspapers, radio and television did not exist then and the people didn't travel often or far, except to Jerusalem for the religious festivals.

The most popular and best-attended celebration of the year was the Jewish Passover feast. It was held in memory of the exodus of Israel from Egypt—almost thirteen hundred years before the time of Christ (Exodus 12).

Jesus and His disciples made their journey to Jerusalem like any respectable decent Jew did. The Passover feast usually fell in April or the beginning of May. The date is very comparable to the time of Easter in our culture today.

At the time of the Passover feast the Jews not only came from the entire country but also from foreign places to show their loyalty and to pay their dues to God. The Temple tax of half a shekel was only part of the offering they brought (Exodus 30:12-16). Many sacrifices were offered during that time and free-will gifts laid into the Temple treasury to "buy" God's favor and blessing. The more that was paid and done, the better the Jewish leaders and scribes liked it. It made them rich!

No Roman money could be brought into the Temple.

Roman coins bore the image of Caesar (Matthew 22:19-21). The Jews didn't believe in making *any* pictures or images of anything or anybody (Exodus 20:4). So all the foreign money had to be exchanged for temple money, and the Romans only allowed temple money for such a use. The Jews were not permitted to use their own coins for any trade.

The Jewish money-changers were in all possibility as corrupt as the system they worked for. They most likely set their own exchange rate and robbed the worshipers as they pleased. Maybe they shared their profit with the priests.

People who came from a great distance couldn't bring their own sacrificial animals along. So they bought what they needed in the outer Temple court, which was called the Court of the Gentiles. Animals which were brought were often rejected by the priests as imperfect and with a blemish. So the people had to buy another one from the Temple market anyway.

Since the religious leaders laid very heavy requirements upon the people, it was often impossible for the poor to comply with all that was demanded of them. How everyone must have longed to find a new way to God's forgiveness and mercy. How hopeless it must have looked for many, especially the poor.

The outer court was turned into a marketplace where cattle lowed, sheep bleated and doves fluttered and cooed. Money-changers outscreamed each other. People thronged around trying to find the best bargain.

The pungent odor of burning animal fat and warm blood indicated that the priests were slaughtering animal after animal in a ritual of sacrifices which had lost their meaning. The faithful worshipers had been told that they must sacrifice and pay in order to receive God's blessing upon themselves and the fruit of their land. So they tried. Oh, how they tried!

Into this scene steps Jesus Christ! Nobody in Jerusalem knew Him. Very few had heard of Him, ever. (Bible scholars usually put this event into the spring of A.D. 27.) A carpenter's son, in the humble clothes of Galilee, He stands at the entrance of the outer court and looks. He takes some cords, used to tie down cattle, and makes a whip for His strong, calloused carpenter's hand. His voice fills the court when He gives a clear command, "Get out of here! You are making My Father's prayer house, a market place" (John 2:16)!

He helps His words along by chasing the cattle, the sellers and the money-changers out while, at the same time, scattering the coins and overturning the money tables.

It is understandable that Christ would do such a thing. The disciples understood and thought of it as a fulfillment of a well-known prophecy: "The zeal of thine house hath eaten me up (Psalm 69:9, *KJV*).

What is hard to understand (because the Bible tells so few details) is why the enterprising merchants and money-changers left their money and ran. Why did a whole court full of people obey an unknown, simply-dressed peasant man who raised His whip and voice?

In order to comprehend that moment fully one must look behind and beyond the physical happenings of the Temple scene. Christ's life was, from the moment of His earthly conception, a controversy and in conflict not with flesh and blood alone but with the evil superpowers under heaven (Ephesians 6:12).

Shortly before He walked into the Temple to perform His first act which would make Him nationally known, He had gone through the sufferings of Satan's three overpowering temptations. Christ defeated the arch-tempter while heaven and hell watched. The evil spirits trembled as they saw the human Christ win every round over their devilish master. They realized that One had arrived who had greater power than even Satan, the "prince of the earth" (John 12:31) had.

When Jesus stepped into the Temple court and raised the whip in His hand, the demons scrambled and fled. Satan and his angels always flee when Divine Presence is around. They cannot and will not stay when God is in a place. Satan is a coward and fights dirty, and he will not stand by his followers in trouble; he is the first one to run. When the demonic spirits left the Temple court, the backbone of those who served Satan in greed and deceit crumbled too. They ran in panic, knowing in their hearts that the Man with the whip spoke the truth. Priests, merchants, cattle, doves all left immediately—and most likely without protest and resistance. The Jews knew only too well that any commotion or riot-like appearance would swiftly bring the Romans down from the Fortress of Antonia at the northern edge of the Temple area. The Roman watchtowers rose high above the Temple and Roman soldiers alertly watched the place at all times. They probably stood double-duty on Jewish holy days when revolts and protests could be expected at the smallest provocation.

So the leaders didn't argue with the Stranger. He walked in as if He owned the place and acted as if He had official authority to administer over the affairs of the Temple. They didn't dare do anything. They were afraid of the Romans who never asked *who* caused a riot, but gathered all the people up and mercilessly punished everyone they caught. Though the Bible does not give us the vivid details, it is also safe to assume that Christ's face and appearance blazed with such power and holy indignation that everyone felt condemned by His ardor and zeal for His "Father's house."

We don't know how long the Temple courts stayed empty and silent. It must have been a relief for the many worshipers to bow before their God in reverence and silence. Maybe they felt near to God in a new way in the presence of the One who perhaps Himself, with His disciples, bowed in prayer after the Temple was cleansed.

Slowly the Temple courts must have filled again. The Jewish leaders and priests returned. They asked Jesus a question (John 2:18). The nature of their question gives us deep insight into their thinking. They obviously knew the true function and purpose for which the Temple had been dedicated (Exodus 25:8,9; Isaiah 56:7). They couldn't argue about that. But Christ had challenged their authority. The Jewish leaders were in charge of the place. No common man dared to question their total command and right to lord it over everyone with regard to the religious affairs of the entire nation.

"What's your authority?" they asked, still scared, but haughty and contemptuous. "Give us a sign."

Christ's answer shows us the spirit in which the question was posed and what He thought of it. Knowing that the Jews ignored the sign they had just witnessed—how by divine power and without ever using the whip He had swept out all the courts of the outer Temple area—Jesus refused to put on a "show" for them to prove His right and authority. If they sincerely were seeking a true answer, they could have recognized His announcement of His messianic mission. He made it clear that it was *His* Father's house that He was clearing out and preparing for true worship.

Jesus saw the hate in the eyes of those who challenged Him. He knew already where it all would soon end. He knew before He walked down to the Jordan to be baptized that He was on the way to a cross. He also knew that after the bitter human end and His humiliating death He would be resurrected and gain complete victory over Satan and his human instruments. Christ looked nearly three years ahead when He said, "Destroy this temple, and in three days I will raise it up" (John 2:19). I wonder, did He point at Himself when He said it?

We know that He did not refer to the outer Temple area when He answered. The Bible word used to tell about the story of the cleansing of the Temple is the Greek word, *hieron*, which means the "courts of the Temple." When Christ said, "Destroy *this* temple," the Bible gives us the Greek word, *naos*, for Christ's Temple. That means the main building which contained the Holy Place and the Holy of Holies.

Nobody understood Christ's answer at the time He said the mysterious words. The religious leaders had no intention to look for any deeper meaning or take it as a divine analogy or prophecy. They had their minds all settled about what to do with this impertinent intruder who blasphemed God by calling Him in a special sense *His* Father.

His answer seemed so absurd! Had not the Temple taken forty-six years to build? Even the disciples puzzled over their Master's answer. Had He not come to be the Deliverer and new King of the Jewish nation? Nobody looked for destruction and breakdown but for fame and new glory.

Nearly three years later Christ's statement was clearly remembered by all those who had heard Him say it. The Jewish leaders used His declaration by distorting it into a charge that He had said *He* would destroy the Temple Himself (Matthew 26:61). The disciples remembered and understood what He meant after His resurrection (John 2:22).

Why did Christ start His ministry by an act which made Him unpopular with the leaders and left His followers puzzled and perplexed? Would it not have been more sensible to start with less controversy?

He did do miracles after the cleansing of the Temple;

the Bible tells us so (John 2:23). But they were done for and among the common people, not for a show or as proof to the Jewish leaders.

We don't know *what* He did. In my mind I can see Him heal all the poor sick people who had come to the Temple for help but couldn't find relief. The priests ignored them because they couldn't pay or buy a sacrifice. The people were desperate and forsaken. Christ brought healing and hope—and many believed in His name (John 2:23).

Christ helped the people but He didn't permit Himself to be fooled by His sudden popularity. He knew human nature too well. He knew the fickleness of human hearts. People are so eager to follow when things go well but He knew that many would leave Him when the going got rough (John 6:64). So He didn't trust Himself to those who professed to believe in Him.

What a lonely way to begin a ministry. What an unusual way Jesus' heavenly Father chose to introduce His beloved Son to a heedless nation. He gave them every possible chance to believe in Him, but He didn't do it the way common human sense would have done it. It was done *God's* way, and His ways are different than ours (Isaiah 55:8,9). In order to believe in Christ people need more than human eyesight; they need to see and ask with the heart.

Only very few people are willing to go so far. It was that way when Jesus walked on this earth personally; it is still that same way today. People run after miracles and excitement but they don't want to bother with true spiritual insights and deep heart searching.

The priests could have known that Christ's answer had special meaning. When He compared Himself to the Temple, He pointed to the fact that the earthly Temple had been designed to be the earthly dwelling place of God (Exodus 25:8,9). Above the mercy seat had appeared in olden days the glory of God's abiding presence (Exodus 25:17). Now, in Christ, the same divine glory dwelled in human flesh in the person of Jesus Christ (John 1:14).

Most people saw only a zealous Galilean peasant making a surprise move and disturbing the business of the Temple, when they could have seen divinity in human garb and welcomed the miracle.

Would it be any different today if Christ walked into many worship services? Would He be welcomed as an honored guest or would He upset the order of service? Would He have to remind us that His church is a "house of prayer," not a place for common things, thoughts, words and actions? (See 1 Corinthians 11:22.)

We wonder how the ancient Jews could have been so slow to understand and "see" Him as their Messiah, but are we not slow to learn ourselves? (See Hebrews 5:12-14.)

LET'S PRAY: Dear Father in heaven, I know that my body became a temple when I was born into the family of God. You dwell in me through the Holy Spirit with Your glory. I wonder if I need a good temple cleansing? If I do, please Jesus, come in and throw out what does not belong in me. If there is any greed, envy, gossip, lust or other sin, drive it out even if it came in under the disguise of religious service. I want to be a "house of prayer" for our heavenly Father and for You, dear Lord. Come and clean up—and keep me clean. I cannot do it myself but only through You, dear Jesus, and for Your sake. Amen.

13
JESUS SEES THE HEART

We do not know when Nicodemus came to see Jesus by night, but we can assume that it happened soon after the first cleansing of the Temple and after the time of miracles when many began to believe (John 2:23).

Nicodemus was a Jewish leader and most likely a member of the Sanhedrin and a Pharisee. He had adopted a Greek name that meant, "conqueror of the people." The Bible does not tell us how he heard about Jesus. One can only wonder: did he watch Him cleanse the Temple? Did he see the Lord do some miracle and watch the sick walk away, healed and praising God?

We don't know how it all started. But we know that Nicodemus came to the young Galilean teacher by night. The reason was obvious. He didn't want to compromise his well-known and respected position by being seen with a questionable upstart whom the Jewish leadership rejected from the beginning. Nicodemus wasn't too eager to be teased or rebuked in the Sanhedrin for making a fool of himself. Nevertheless something bothered the good man enough that he broke the Roman curfew to find some needed answers. He took a risk and met with Jesus of Nazareth under the cover of darkness.

Nicodemus must have conquered people with graciousness. He knew how to be polished and polite, and he treated the young peasant fellow from up north with great benevolence. He even went so far as to address Him as *Rabbi*, which means teacher. It was a most honored title and Nicodemus knew it. He was also a "master of Israel." When he acknowledged Jesus as his equal, he really outdid himself. Jesus had no formal education and no official permission by the Sanhedrin to teach. But Nicodemus was willing to grant that Jesus had something to say worth hearing.

Nicodemus hid his uncertainty behind flowery speech, but Jesus saw his heart. And Nicodemus came with a deep longing and honest searching, though he couldn't admit it at first (John 3:2).

Jesus didn't bother to react to the flattering introduction. He *knew* the man's heart and He answered Nicodemus' unspoken question before His visitor had the courage to admit his confusion.

"Verily, verily," Jesus said (John 3:3). The word, verily, is used by Christ through the entire New Testament and always signifies statements of special truth. The double form is seldom used by anyone else at the beginning of a sentence, only by the Lord Himself.

"These are not speculations but most important principles of truth," Christ indicated by His introduction. "You must be born again or you can't see the kingdom of God" (John 3:3).

Nicodemus couldn't believe his ears. Was this young Galilean telling him that he, Nicodemus, did *not* have a sure guarantee of admission into the kingdom of heaven? According to Jewish theology, to be of the seed of Abraham entitled a man to favor with God and entrance to the eternal kingdom. It was a known fact that non-Jews had to go through a special adoption ceremony to become sons of Abraham in order to make it to heaven, but that any full-blooded Jew would have to worry about his salvation seemed hard to believe.

Jesus knew the sore spot in the heart of Nicodemus and gently He laid His finger on it. He knew that His visitor would have to move the pride of his heritage first in order to see new light.

Nicodemus was so eager and willing to learn that he humbled himself to the point where he admitted that he didn't have the answer to everything. He simply didn't understand: "How can that be?" he said, subdued (John 3:4,9).

Jesus had to reproach him but He did it ever so tactfully and full of love. "How can you call yourself a teacher and not understand the basic principles of spiritual and heavenly things?" Christ said kindly and proceeded to explain the things of the Spirit to him (John 3:8).

As we read this short story about the visit between the two teachers of Israel, and follow their conversation, we can learn many things from our Lord. Jesus accepted people where they were. He didn't demand understanding or become impatient and defensive with someone who couldn't grasp the new light immediately. Patiently He worked with the man's own frame of reference, not with His own.

"Look," Jesus said, "you are very familiar with the books of Moses and know the story of the brazen serpent well. Remember *all* the people had to do was to *look* and they could live (Numbers 21:9). You think that you can earn your way to heaven—by heritage, good works, fulfilling of your many laws and other right deeds—but that is not so. It is much simpler, so simple in fact that it offends your educated intellect."

Then Christ did something that overwhelms me every time I think about it. Jesus made a statement—the most famous statement He ever made while He lived on our earth: "For God so loved the world, that he gave his only begotten Son, that whosoever believeth in him should not perish, but have everlasting life" (John 3:16).

This sentence is the greatest sermon ever preached—and when it was said for the first time, Jesus said it to *one* person. He didn't wait until He gathered a crowd of several thousand people together to make such a magnificent statement. He could have watched the impact go like a ripple from person to person and know He had scored as a preacher. But Jesus didn't need a crowd to wax eloquent. One human soul was so important to Him that He shared one of His greatest gems of truth, under the cover of darkness, with one lone man who was actually ashamed of Him.

But what Jesus said to him that night was never lost. Nicodemus hid all the words of the Lord in his heart and must have later shared them with John, the Lord's beloved disciple. Through his Gospel it came down to us. Through the ages, millions have been transformed by that message—just like Nicodemus.

The Bible mentions Nicodemus after that visit only two other times. One time was when he defended Jesus before the Sanhedrin (John 7:50-52). He obviously never stepped out and became a known disciple of Christ but he used his influence to thwart the plans of those who tried to kill Jesus before the appointed time.

The next time Scripture mentions Nicodemus is in John 19:38-42. While he was a secret follower of Jesus as long as He lived on earth, Nicodemus came out and confessed His full allegiance to Christ at our Lord's darkest hour. When the disciples fled and the cause looked hopeless because Jesus' body hung limp and dead on a cross, Nicodemus came and helped to bury Him. He probably used his own burial spices to wrap the bruised form tenderly, and he and Joseph of Arimathea might have personally carried Him into the tomb (John 19:42). By this act they defiled themselves and knew they would not be able to take part in the Temple services of the Passover the next day. Since the Passover was by far the most important ceremony for any pious Jew, we can know that Nicodemus must have had a change of heart. He obviously had learned and understood by then Christ's teaching of the brazen serpent and the true way of salvation.

We never hear anything more of Nicodemus in the Bible, but we can be sure that he has found his way to heaven.

That Jesus always looks at the heart and is never a respector of persons is shown in another story where again He had a very unusual encounter. This time it is not a highly respected Jewish leader that Jesus visits, but a Samaritan woman (John 4:3-29).

In order to understand the significance of this story, we must first of all know the Jewish customs of Christ's time with regard to women. A woman at that time was not regarded as a person but as property bought by a man. A woman's place was in the home. A Jewish man *never* spoke to a woman unless he was related to her. A rabbi would never speak to *any* Jewish woman in public, not even those of his own household.

Christ had established His reputation as a rabbi by the time He and His disciples left Judea to go back to Galilee. In the process of the journey they had to pass "through Samaria" (John 4:4). Now the Jews despised the Samaritans. They thought of them as half-breeds who had intermarried with Gentiles. For more than five hundred years before Christ's time they had no dealings with these second-class people. A devout Jew would not even cross their land when traveling between Judea and Galilee, but would take the long way around.

But Christ passed *through* it. The Bible says He had to—to meet *one* person! She wasn't regarded as a person, not even among the Samaritans. Not only was she a woman, she was a social outcast with a bad reputation. She came to the well for water at a time when nobody else was around, in the heat of the noon day. The rest of the village women came at the customary time, in the early morning or late afternoon.

When she arrived at Jacob's well, one lone weary traveler sat at the curbstone. It was obvious that He was a Jew. He would ignore her, act as if she didn't even exist. She knew this and expected nothing else. The last thing she would have thought of was His friendly request, "Give Me to drink" (John 4:7).

She was so startled that she didn't hand Him any water but asked a question, "Why would you, being a Jew, ask *me* for a drink" (John 4:9)?

A devout Jew would rather have suffered thirst than ask her. She knew that only too well. Jesus was weary and thirsty, but it is obvious in the later part of the story that He didn't ask for the water to meet His own physical needs but to meet her need of a Saviour.

How thoughtful, kind and generous of Him! How well He knew how to reach the heart of any human being. By asking her to do a favor for Him, He broke down prejudice and resentment. If He had offered her a favor first, she could have rejected it. She could have felt like a dog who received some crumbs from a superior being and chosen to ignore it. She could not refuse His request of her for water. In her part of the world a plea for water is sacred; it cannot even be denied to an enemy.

When Jesus asked *her* for water, He did something else. He declared His respect for her. He honored her as a person and ignored the fact that not only was she a Samaritan but a woman on top of that.

Now, if He had known what *kind* of an immoral woman she was, He would have never spoken one word; that she knew for sure! But He *did* know and He told her so. His tactfulness and tender care not to hurt her feelings shall be forever a living example to His disciples and followers. He wasn't blunt. He did not expose and condemn. Gently He awakened in her a new desire for something better. Conviction of her need for spiritual things followed and she knew she had to make a decision. She could either believe this stranger at the well or reject Him.

As we read their conversation, we find Jesus teaching her a truth similar to that which He taught Nicodemus. He explains the need for spiritual renewal to find salvation. But He changed His approach, His way of teaching and the examples He used in order to meet her on her own ground. Had He explained it to her the way He had taught Nicodemus she would never have understood it. And Nicodemus would have rejected the Lord's teaching if He had said to him what He said to the woman. Christ knew and knows the heart of a person. He *never* judges on outward appearance. How comforting and how solemn a lesson to learn.

The disciples were much slower to learn than the little despised woman who was considered an evil prostitute by her society. As the disciples came back from the village, where they had bought food for themselves and their Master, they couldn't believe their eyes and ears. Had Jesus forgotten all decent rules of good behavior?

No, He had not! He had come to earth to break down social barriers and prejudices and teach the *true* value of a human soul.

The thirst in the woman's soul was quenched. In one quick moment she became a new person when she looked beyond the weary, dust-covered traveler and saw the Messiah as He said to her, "I who speak unto thee am He."

The social outcast who walked to the well in stifling midday heat to avoid the scorning frowns and disapproving looks of the decent women of her village, left her water pot and walked right back into town. Was she so excited that she forgot her pots? Was she so eager that she didn't want to be slowed down for the things she intended to do? Did she leave the pot so the Master and the disciples could draw water and drink their fill? One thing is sure, by leaving her pots behind she was saying, "I'll be back!"

And she came back, but not alone. She brought with her those she had talked to, the *men* of her city. She broke the custom of her time when she spoke to the men—but they were obviously the only ones who would even give her a chance to tell her story. The women wouldn't have listened to her.

Who was *she* to tell anyone that she had met a prophet, perhaps the Messiah? The men knew that something extraordinary had happened when they looked into her glowing face. She didn't prance and flirt or keep her head down in shame; she had something important to tell and she shared the good news (John 4:29).

She was so convincing that they followed her out to the well and got acquainted with the visitor. They urged Him to stay with them awhile and He accepted the invitation. For two days He stayed and taught and when He and His disciples finally had to leave, He left behind the first group of converts who believed in Him as the Christ, the Saviour of the *world*, not only of the Jews (John 4:42).

The disciples of Jesus must have watched the whole happening with mixed feelings. On the one hand they watched their Master break every law of Jewish society when He not only spoke to a Samaritan woman but also stayed in Samaria overnight for social interaction and friendly visiting. On the other hand they couldn't deny the fact that the Samaritans were much more willing and ready to accept Christ's teaching than the Jews in Judea.

The Samaritans did not demand a "sign" as the Jewish leaders did. Jesus did not have to be as reserved and careful when He taught them either. He could be honest and say as He did to the woman, "I am the Messiah you have been waiting for!" The Samaritans accepted Him because they heard *Him*, not because they listened to the woman's slightly exaggerated statement that "He told me *all* things that I ever did" (John 4:29).

Whenever faith in Christ is built on His Word alone and not on any outward appearance (be it for or against Him) then such faith can grow and mature and bring a great harvest of souls.

The Lord never needs crowds or a big "show." He needs *one* willing person in *any* social class and He can begin a work that can grow and spread forever.

LET'S PRAY: Dear Jesus, sometimes I wonder what *one* person can do for You and I think of myself. I feel so unimportant, misunderstood, often rejected, and I am not too proud of my past either.

Help me to understand that it isn't my status or social standing that You need or want. You long for me as a person. I keep forgetting. It's not my ability but my availability that counts.

Lord, help me not only to make myself available to You, but protect me from judging. I don't know hearts as You do, Lord, so often I jump to the wrong conclusions as I see only the outward appearance. Teach me to see the heart as You did. Help me to become as tender, tactful and gentle as You are that I may lead sinners and saints to You, for both need You. Nicodemus and the woman at the well stood on opposite sides of society, but you treated both of them with the same love and compassion. Please, Jesus, show me Your way to human hearts that I may follow Your example. For Your love's sake. Amen.

14
A PROPHET IN HIS OWN COUNTRY

Bible scholars do not agree when the happenings in the synagogue of Nazareth took place which we read of in the Gospel of Luke (Luke 4:16-30). It is generally believed that Jesus, after crossing Samaria, returned from Judea to His hometown and went on the Sabbath to the synagogue to worship, as was His custom (Luke 4:16).

The Jewish synagogue at Christ's time was the center of all community life. It directed the religious and intellectual activity for every pious household. Everyone attended Sabbath morning worship in the synagogue every week. The men sat or stood in the men's section while the women and children worshiped on the opposite side.

The Temple in Jerusalem had to be visited three times a year. The rest of the time the Jews assembled in the "house of prayer," or "assembly." No sacrifices were slaughtered there. The congregation gathered for prayer, read the Scripture, performed rites, sang and received instruction.

The high point in the weekly Sabbath morning service was reached with the public reading of the *Siddur* (the prayer book) and the weekly portion from the Torah. This was followed by the reading of applicable selections from the *Haftorah* (the prophetic writings). Often the reader, who was called the "dismisser," gave his remarks and exhortations based on the passage which then closed the service.

The ruler of the synagogue who presided with the

board of elders, appointed suitable men from the congregation to pray, read the Scriptures and exhort the congregation. There were no assigned "clergy" and the Temple priests were not automatically the leaders of their synagogues, though they were highly respected. Anyone could pray and read if He was of good reputation. Visiting rabbis got invited to take part in the service. When Christ came home His family and neighbors had heard about His new fame and reputation. Therefore after the Torah had been read the *chazzan* (deacon) handed Jesus the scroll of Isaiah. We do not know if there were assigned prophetic readings for each week or if the reader could choose his own portion of Scripture. We know that Jesus unrolled the scroll—re-rolling it with His other hand—until He found Isaiah 61, verses 1 and 2. (According to the Dead Sea Scrolls found in modern times that portion of the book would have been almost at the end of the scroll.)

He read the familiar words but stopped in the middle of a sentence with, "to preach the acceptable year of the Lord." He did not read "and the day of vengeance of our God" (Isaiah 61:2).

Custom required the reader to stand for the public reading of the Law and the Prophets. For the teaching and exhortation which followed the reading, the man sat down in a special seat, often called "the chair of Moses." It stood on a raised platform near the lectern. The scrolls themselves were kept in a cart called an ark and were only brought out for the actual time of reading.

So Jesus handed the scroll back to the servant who put it back into the ark and then Jesus sat down to teach.

Jewish teaching has always consisted of quoting great rabbis of the past. It is still customary today in any Jewish synagogue of modern times. In Jesus' time the two most quoted rabbis were men by the names of Hillel and Shammai. Hillel was considered the greater of the two according to the following ancient record:

A heathen once came to Rabbi Shammai and stated: "I'll accept the Jewish religion if you can teach me the entire law (Torah) while standing on one leg."

Shammai grabbed a rod and drove the rude heathen out of his house.

So the heathen visited Rabbi Hillel and stated the same thing.

Hillel smiled and said gently, "Do not unto others what you do not wish that others do unto you. That *is* the whole Torah. Everything else is only commentary. Go and learn!"

As it was mentioned earlier (chapter 6), Hillel was still alive during Jesus' childhood days. It is easy to assume that Jesus might have listened to his teachings. Jesus knew well the method of Jewish teaching since it was His custom to attend synagogue services regularly, most likely from childhood on. It is also clear that Jesus spoke Hebrew and Aramaic fluently. The Scripture was always read in Hebrew then translated into Aramaic, which was a mixture of simple Hebrew and Greek. It was the only language understood by the common people. The teaching was done in Aramaic. So, after the Hebrew reading was finished, every eye was on the Lord Jesus (Luke 4:20). Suspense filled the air. What would He do? Would He begin His sermon with a spectacular miracle? Would He announce that the time had come to drive the Romans out? Would He quote Hillel?

We do not know all that He said, but the first part of His sermon was well-liked. The people were fascinated by His gracious words of wisdom and wondered: "Is this not Joseph's son?" Though Jesus had never been adopted by Joseph, people in His hometown associated the two together and He simply was "the carpenter's son" (Luke 4:22). When His neighbors began to ask *that* question, a question of doubt, Satan got into their hearts with negative thoughts and more doubts. They simply refused to admit that Jesus could possibly be *more* than what He had been among them, a poor peasant man who grew up in their midst.

Jesus knew the hearts of men again. He probably answered their unspoken secret thought when He said, "Today the Scripture has been fulfilled in your ears and hearing" (Luke 4:21).

The Jews have always regarded Isaiah 61:1 and 2 as a clear Messianic prophecy and they understood what Jesus said. He not only had the audacity in their eyes to quote Himself as an authority in His own right, (He enraged many Jews through His entire ministry by saying, "You have heard it said, ... but I say unto you," Matthew 5:21-48), but He actually claimed to be the Messiah! He also indicated that it was they, the Jews, who were bound, blind and broken off. On top of all this He had omitted their favorite part of that passage, the promise of God's vengeance upon the heathen. He actually cited the heathen as being smarter than the Jews and blamed on the condition of their heart the fact that God couldn't do any special thing for them.

The longer the Nazarenes listened, the more upset they got. They stopped listening before Christ stopped speaking—there was no benediction said after His sermon. While "keeping the Law" of the Sabbath, murderous thoughts filled their hearts and their wrath made them determined to destroy the Lord. They dragged Him out to the brow of a hill and tried to push Him over the cliff. (The Mount of Precipitation which is today pointed out as the traditional site of the event is more than two miles from Nazareth. This is much farther than one Sabbath day's journey and the Jews would never have "broken" the Law by walking that far. It is more likely that they found a limestone cliff nearer to town where they tried to get rid of Him.)

But Jesus "passed through the midst of them and went His way" (Luke 4:30). If they could have seen with spiritual eyes, they would have seen God's angels moving the raging crowd apart, making a clear path for the beloved Lord. As long as His time hadn't come, nobody could touch Him (John 7:30).

Physically they couldn't hurt Him but oh how He ached for them in His loving soul! He knew that not even His own brothers believed in Him and the Bible again tells us what His mother Mary must have thought (John 7:5). Maybe she wondered why her son had to aggravate the Jews so badly. Couldn't He have softened His message a bit?

Sure, everyone knew in his heart that Jesus described them rather perfectly, but it wasn't in the Jewish spirit of that time to admit it. Fierce national pride and wrong reasoning closed the doors to repentance and possible change. The crowd stopped yelling and fuming when the "son of Joseph" was all of a sudden gone and they found themselves screaming into the empty air.

Jesus walked away and, probably with a heavy heart, made His way down to Capernaum. Nazareth lies high in the hills; Capernaum is some twenty miles away on the shore of the lake of Galilee. He did there what He did everywhere, He taught the people and they listened with astonishment (Luke 4:32).

Jesus Christ did not teach as everyone else did. He did not follow the custom of His time and quote words of others. He taught with a "power." The Greek word is *excousia*, which means "authority" (Matthew 7:29). He spoke by the authority of God Himself and spoke His own words, not memorized phrases. No doubt Jesus used the well-known phrases and proverbs of His time to lead His listeners along familiar ground, but He had an astonishing way of bringing new life and meaning into old sayings. He even took Hillel's famous statement and turned his negative approach into a positive way of life. "Look," He said in one of His great teaching sessions, "there is nothing wrong with Hillel's teaching and his famous saying, but it works better if you turn it around and you *do* unto others as you want them to do with you" (Matthew 7:12).

It isn't what you don't do that counts. It's what you *do* in love that matters.

Jesus lived what He preached. He loved and longed for His people to see Him for their sake in God's true light. In spite of the rough treatment He had received from His former neighbors and childhood pals in Nazareth, we find Jesus goes back to them for a second time. Bible scholars place His final visit in the winter of A.D. 30-31 (Mark 6:1-5).

He preached again in their synagogue. Didn't Jesus realize that He was wasting His time? They rejected Him again and He couldn't perform a single great miracle because of their unbelief. A few sick people got healed but that was all (Mark 6:5).

Christ didn't do things in human wisdom and understanding. He was led by God every step of the way. God had declared to His chosen people that nobody could be condemned by a single witness alone (Deuteronomy 19:15). Even God would not condemn in the judgment by the witness of His Son alone, but on the evidence of two or three witnesses (John 5:30-47). Jesus Christ pleaded for a second time with the hardened hearts of the people who knew Him so well. But neither His wisdom, which they couldn't deny, nor His fame could make a dent. They refused to believe! He gave them every possible chance but they willed not to accept Him (Mark 6:4,5). Christ wondered at their unbelief. Heaven still wonders at people's willful unbelief today!

Anyone has a chance to see God if he wants to. Nobody has an excuse (Romans 1:20). Christ will send to everyone at least two or three witnesses about His great love. He will make it very hard for anyone to be lost. But if someone closes his eyes in the presence of all the clear evidence, even God Himself cannot or will not force him to find salvation.

For many, Christ has become too familiar because they have grown up in Christian homes and have heard about Him all their lives. He has become a "prophet . . . without honor . . . among His own" (Mark 6:4). They follow the ways of the world because it's a "new" thing. Human nature hasn't changed, has it?

LET'S PRAY: Dear Jesus, it's hard to believe that those who knew You best treated You with such indifference and hate. They should have known better as they watched Your sinless life, even during Your childhood and youth. Your goodness must have irritated them and Your love and kindness exposed the evil in their own dark hearts. I know I have been unfairly attacked by those around me because I try to live a Christian life. But I'd rather suffer a little bit like You did instead of taking You for granted and treating You as too familiar and common.

Lord, may You never become a "prophet . . . without honor" in my life and house. Teach me to revere and honor You as an example to my family and others. To know You is to love You—and I love You very much, my Master and Lord, Jesus Christ. Amen.

15
JESUS CAME TO HEAL

Jesus' first recorded healing miracle happened when He was on His way to Capernaum, perhaps shortly after the people in Nazareth had tried to kill Him. He stopped over in Cana where the people still remembered His very first miracle: the turning of water into wine at the marriage feast. The Galileans had also seen and heard all He had done at the Passover Feast in Jerusalem, and His fame spread before Him. The fact that the Jewish leaders and the people of the south (Judea) hesitated to accept Jesus put Him in favor with the Galileans. Jesus was one of them, and the proud, stuck-up attitude of the Judeans was known and resented in the north. So the Galileans received Him (John 4:45).

In Cana a nobleman from Capernaum came to see Jesus. Nobleman means literally "king's man," which suggests that he was a royal officer, perhaps a court man of Herod Antipas.

The nobleman's son was sick at the point of death (v. 47). The troubled father had come to ask Jesus to go with him to the bedside of the dying boy. It was a trip of sixteen miles from Cana to Capernaum.

Jesus, ever ready to help, did a strange thing. He didn't respond; instead He reproved the anxious father. "Unless you see signs and wonders you don't believe, do you?" (v. 48) the Lord said, and looked into the nobleman's face.

The nobleman knew that the Lord saw his heart and he knew immediately why Jesus said what He did. The nobleman wasn't ready to accept Jesus by simple faith like the despised Samaritans did. He came to Jesus because human help had failed and he had no other place left to go. He wasn't sure if Jesus could heal his son, but in desperation he hoped so! *If* he saw the wonder of healing, he would believe. But God's spiritual laws don't work that way. One believes *first* and the miracle follows, both in the earthly life as well as in the born-again experience (John 4:50,51; 3:16).

The anxious father didn't argue. Maybe he just bowed his head humbly to show that he understood. He had sought out Jesus believing that He would "come down" immediately since it could only be to the young Teacher's advantage to make connections with the upper social class. The nobleman was used to giving orders but he found out that nobody ordered Jesus around except His Father in heaven.

Jesus was never a respector of persons. He neither judged nor helped people according to their social standing but rather according to their hearts. All the father's haughtiness and superior attitude were gone when he cried out in desperation: "Sir [which means Lord], come down ere my child die" (John 4:49)!

Jesus never closes His ear to a humble and honest cry for help. He replied immediately, "Go thy way, thy son liveth." With it He said, "My friend, I cannot be told what to do and I am not coming to your place just because you are an influential man. But if you want to, you can believe Me."

The nobleman believed and started back home. The Bible tells us that the fever left the boy at the moment Christ said, "Thy son liveth." The fever left one hour after midday, when usually a fever is at its peak—in the heat of the day. And the nobleman and his household believed in Jesus, not *after* the son was healed, but the father believed *before* the son was well (v. 50).

We find a similar happening in another healing story in the Gospels of Matthew and Luke (Matthew 8:5-13; Luke 7:1-10).

When Christ visited Capernaum He was approached by a centurion—a Roman officer in command of one hundred men. He was obviously not a Jew but a Gentile. He came to the Lord and asked Him to heal his servant. The sick man was actually a slave or bond slave, but he was very dear to the heathen master.

The Roman sent a Jewish delegation to give Jesus his request. Jesus said, "I will come and heal him" (Luke 7:3-6)! The entire group set out for the centurion's house. Before Jesus got there the centurion met Him on the road and said humbly, "Lord, I am not worthy that You step under my roof. Just say the word and my servant will be healed" (vv. 6,7).

The centurion respected the Jewish code of ethics which forbade a Jew to step into a Gentile's house. Because he was a Roman officer he knew that he could just snap a finger and give an order to bring Jesus to his house. But instead he humbly put himself below the Jews and the famous Rabbi Jesus.

Jesus marveled at the faith of that heathen Roman and said, "I haven't found such faith among the Jews anywhere" (v. 9). The centurion's request was granted and the slave got well immediately.

One wonders, why did Jesus refuse to go to the nobleman's house but started out at once for the centurion's house? Why did He meet the Jewish leader with a reproach but set the Roman up as an example?

The difference lies in the faith of the two individuals. The centurion trusted Jesus implicitly but the nobleman set limits. Faith makes the difference. That "spiritual law" is demonstrated in every healing miracle recorded in the Bible.

One of my favorite stories that proves God's point

about faith is the one about the woman who was healed of a blood disease. It was so dramatic that three Gospel writers report it (Matthew 9:20-22; Mark 5:25-34; Luke 8:43-48).

The woman had been afflicted with an incurable sickness for twelve long years. Not only had she spent all her money on doctors and only gotten worse but the constant flow of blood had made her weak and an outcast of society. According to Jewish law she was unclean and not permitted to touch or mingle with people (Leviticus 15:19-28). The Bible calls her sickness a "plague," in Greek *mastix*, which means "a whip" or "a scourge." In Jewish thinking those with incurable afflictions were commonly thought of as being divinely punished for sins in their parents' lives.

The woman most likely did not dare to come up and speak to the Lord. A Jewish woman never addressed a Jewish man first, even if she was not unclean at that moment. In this woman's case she was both—a woman and unclean. "If I only could touch the hem of His garment," she thought. And then she did just that while the crowd pressed around Jesus. She reached out and touched Him (Mark 5:27,28).

"Who touched Me?" Jesus asked.

The woman trembled in fear for touching Jesus made Him—a famous rabbi—also unclean for the day. He was not allowed to touch her either, and He was on His way to look after the daughter of a very important man of the community (Mark 5:22-24). It was bad enough for everyone to know that she, a decent Jewish woman, had touched a strange Jewish man. But now everyone would know about her impurities, and she had no right to even be in a crowd where someone might touch her or where she might contact anyone by accident (Leviticus 15:19).

"Who touched Me?" Jesus asked. And the disciples, who always saw things very sensibly from the human standpoint, began to straighten the Lord's thinking out.

"Everybody is pushing and shoving You, Lord," they said, "what are you talking about" (Mark 5:31)?

"Virtue [power] has gone out of Me," the Lord said and looked around to find her.

The woman shook in fear, but she came forward and threw herself at His feet. If the crowd got angry at her, they could stone her for her improper behavior. Would Christ reverse the miracle if He found out? She told the truth and put herself at His mercy.

Everyone listened and Jesus said, "Daughter!" With that word He said, "You are not a social outcast, you are related officially in the Jewish family. Daughter, *thy faith* has made you whole, go in peace" (v. 34)!

It was important to Christ to teach a lesson to the woman as well as to those around Him. It was not a touch of superstition that made her whole, it was the touch of *faith*! His garment didn't heal the lady, He did. Many others had "touched" Him that day, deliberately or by accident, and nothing happened. But when the woman touched Him *in faith* she was healed. When one comes in contact with Jesus and takes Him for granted, or accepts it as a common thing, nothing will ever happen. But when one comes in faith—then His power is activated. Faith must be in Jesus Christ Himself, not in His miracles, not in the clothing He wore and not even in a nail that pierced His hands later on the cross. Superstition and faith often can be very similar—we must be careful not to confuse them.

Some people may have thought the woman was "out of place," that she acted too presumptuously, but Jesus labeled her action faith and honored it (Mark 5:34).

Another incident of "presumptious" faith took place when Jesus crossed the border into Phoenicia (Mark 7:24-30). This was one of the very few times that Christ and His disciples left the land of Israel and visited some bordering heathen lands. He went there to rest, not to preach (v. 24). The time hadn't yet come to bring the Messianic message to the non-Jews. As much as Christ's heart must have longed to reveal Himself to the whole world, He couldn't do it if He wanted to work with any measure of success among His own people. If He had gone against *all* rules of the Jewish society at this time by ministering to the Gentiles, He would have destroyed His influence with the very people He came to save.

The woman of Canaan was a Greek, a Syrophoenician. She found Jesus in His seclusion and threw herself at His feet (v. 25), the customary Eastern position when presenting a petition to a superior. She must have had some knowledge of Jewish culture and had heard enough about Jesus to know what she was attempting to do. We don't know how she came by such special knowledge but she addressed Him as "Son of David," which was a recognition of Him as the Messiah. She pleaded with Him for her demon-possessed daughter. She asked for healing (v. 26).

Jesus didn't answer her. That was in harmony with Jewish tradition, for the woman had broken many customary rules of social interaction.

First she had the presumption to address a man. A woman always waited to be spoken to. The woman with the blood disease waited until Christ asked, "Who touched Me?" before she answered.

Not only did this woman overstep her boundary as a woman but also as a foreigner, a Gentile. A Jewish rabbi would never even let on that he had noticed her.

Christ acted "right" in the eyes of the people. Since the woman didn't leave when He ignored her, the disciples told Jesus to send her away by a command. She was drawing undesired attention to the group and the disciples were not too eager that it be known in Israel that they had gone into a heathen land. They were in hiding and would like to keep it that way.

Jesus did speak to her, but not as the disciples suggested. "Look," He said to the pleading woman, "I was sent to the children of Israel."

The woman persisted because Jesus had encouraged her—He bothered to talk to her and His words were neither impatient nor unkind, we can be sure of that. As she kept on pleading, He said, "It is not proper to take the children's bread and give it to little dogs" (v. 27).

The Gentile woman never flinched. She detected a compassion behind those seemingly harsh words and she didn't argue the point. She knew that she was nothing in the eyes of the Jews and she accepted it. But she hoped for mercy. Her answer was remarkable: "You are right, Lord," she said, "but even the dogs have a right to the little morsels or crumbs the master tosses to them here and there" (v. 28)!

Jesus rejoiced over this presumptious woman's answer. There is no doubt that He put on this act of resistance to give His prejudiced disciples a firsthand object lesson. He recognized a firm faith in this Syrophoenician woman that didn't falter even when He tested her. And her beautiful humble answer showed that she had passed the test. He honored her (v. 29); when the woman returned to her daughter's bedside she found the girl free of demons (v. 30).

As we read in the New Testament about the many acts of Christ's healings (and not all of them are recorded for a thousand books couldn't tell everything about Him—see John 21:25), we discover some things. There are two common denominators in all the stories—faith and asking. Someone has to have faith to start out with, and the person who has the faith does the asking! The request doesn't always come from the one who needs the healing. Often the sick person receives the benefit of someone else's faith-filled request: fathers and mothers asking for their children; masters asking for their servants; four men asking for their paralytic friend. Jesus healed them all because He saw the faith of the askers.

It must have been spectacular to watch Jesus heal so many broken bodies, but eternity will show His greatest healing miracles are when He healed ever so slowly the broken hearts and the sinsick souls! He is still doing the same thing today, for when Jesus saves He heals.

LET'S PRAY: Precious Lord and great Healer of mankind, I thank You that You didn't stop Your healing power when You left this planet. You are still working the way You did while walking the earth. Sometimes You choose to heal slowly, and once in a while You do a spectacular thing, but it's always the same healing power at work. How I thank You that Your love and care have sustained me for so many years! I am so glad You are not partial, that *anyone* who believes and asks, receives from You. I would be in bad shape if You only listened to the call of important and famous people. I am neither!

So I *believe*, dear Lord, and I am coming near to touch the hem of Your garment, for I am not worthy to do anything else. Do to me as You see best, and I thank You, whatever happens to my body and soul, I am in Your hands. Amen.

16
JESUS CAME TO BRING LIFE

Jesus did not only come to heal, His love and power even brought some people back from physical death and the grave. The Gospel writers tell us about three different people who were raised to new life by the Lord's command.

In Jesus' day there were certain customs that had to be observed whenever a person was nearing death. Flute players and mourners were hired to stay close by. Then when the dying person breathed his last breath, loud wailing and mournful flute melodies announced to the neighbors that death had entered a house. The dead body was immediately washed and prepared for the funeral which had to take place the same day.

Spices and ointments, gathered during the dead person's entire lifetime, were brought forth and the body was anointed. Next, the clothed body was wrapped with white strips of linen—around each limb and around the trunk up to the neck. The arms and legs were tied with bands. The face was not wrapped but was covered with a cloth.

Pallbearers laid the wrapped body on a bier, which most likely was woven of wicker, like a basket. With the flute players and wailing professional mourners leading the way, the sobbing family followed. The neighbors then formed a procession and watched until the body was placed in the tomb, usually a cave, not a hole in the ground. Large wheellike stones were rolled in place to close the entrance to the tomb and the outside was whitewashed to mark it as a grave.

Anyone who touched a dead person or anything around him—clothes, bed, etc.—was declared unclean in ceremonial defilement for seven days (Numbers 19: 11). To be declared unclean was a difficult handicap. Anything an unclean person touched became unclean too. Anyone who was touched by an unclean person became unclean and also had to go through a purification process (Numbers 19:22). So an unclean person had to stay away from everybody and everything—exiled and completely isolated.

Death therefore brought not only heartbreak and sorrow but also great social inconvenience to a devout Jewish family. God gave these wise rules to Israel in Moses' time for the sake of hygiene in the wilderness where primitive living conditions and water scarcity demanded it. What a pity that these rules were still observed during Christ's time and, for the sake of Pharasaic legalism, become an extra burden for those in deep bereavement.

The Gospel writer Luke tells about the time Jesus brought the young man of Nain back to life. Since Luke was a physician, he recorded much about disease and death in his Gospel and often goes into greater detail than the other Gospel writers.

The day after Jesus healed the servant of the centurion, He went to Nain, and many disciples and people went with Him (Luke 7:11). This town is not mentioned elsewhere but it is believed to be the same place as Nein of today. It is situated twenty-five miles southwest of the site of ancient Capernaum and about five miles south of Nazareth. Half a mile east of the village is a rock-hewn burial ground still in use today. As the Lord and His large company came near the gate of the city, they watched a funeral procession approaching them. The story told to them was heartrending (v. 12).

The only son of a widow had died. He was probably in his early teens and was her sole support. He was all she had on this earth and now she would have to go begging, for nobody looked after widows at that time but their own kin (Deuteronomy 25). It was such a tragic loss that many people of the area joined the funeral procession to show their deep sympathy (Luke 7:12).

Jesus looked at the heartbroken mother, dressed in the customary white mourning clothes, and His loving heart overflowed with compassion. He knew she had no hope left in her heart and no faith in Him. She was filled with agony and despair. No words of request came from her mouth. She probably was so occupied with her deep sorrow that she didn't even notice what was going on. She might have had only one recurring petition in her desperate mind and heart: "God, please don't forsake me. What will happen to me now? I am so alone, so very alone."

Christ's love and pity were enough at that moment to answer the unuttered prayer of a despondent human being. "Stop weeping," He said to the crying woman. I can see her look up surprised into His kind face and wonder what He meant. He raised His hand and touched the bier. Most likely it was a gesture that indicated the halt of the procession, both theirs and His.

That one touch rendered Jesus unclean for the next seven days and everybody knew it. I can picture Peter shaking his impatient head and thinking, "What did He do *that* for? It's messing up things for a whole week for all of us!"

But the One who carried life within Himself (John 1:4) and who had come to conquer sin and death (1 Corinthians 15:54-57) could not be defiled by a dead corpse. He spoke a simple clear command, "Young man to *you* I say, arise" (Luke 7:14)!

The dead body moved and sat up. The young man looked into the tearstained face of his mother, and began to talk. Jesus took his arm and led him gently to the speechless, overwhelmed mother and I can see them falling into each other's arms, weeping with joy.

The whole incident happened so fast, and without any pompous show, that the people in the funeral procession and those following Jesus couldn't believe their eyes. At first it scared them; fear seized them (v. 16). Then what actually had happened slowly began to sink in and the people began praising God. The funeral procession dissolved. The hired mourners and flute players went their way. There was nobody left to bury. People went home to tell the story and the exciting news spread all over Galilee and south throughout Judea. We can be sure that even the Jewish leaders and the upper social class heard about it, for shortly after that a Jewish ruler approached the Lord (Luke 8:41).

The man must have been in utter desperation. His only daughter was sick. Doctor Luke again emphasizes that the ruler's *only* daughter was sick, just as he told about the *only* son of the widow. When an *only* child died or was at the point of death, the sorrow of the loss was always multiplied by the tragedy of a family's extinction. It was a cause of great shame and an obvious sign of divine punishment when a family had to die out for lack of an heir. A daughter couldn't carry on the family name but at least she kept the family line alive. And there was always hope that she might be chosen to become the mother of the expected Messiah.

Jairus was most likely the ruler of the synagogue in Capernaum. The proud rabbi was desperate enough and loved his daughter so much that he threw himself at Jesus' feet. By this he acknowledged that Jesus was higher in authority than himself, and he was a respected leader of the Jewish community (v. 41).

"Please, come right away," he pleaded. "My child is almost dead, but if You touch her she will be healed and can live" (Mark 5:22,23)!

Jesus didn't argue or delay. He went with Jairus toward his house. But it was slow going. Too many people thronged and crowded the narrow pathway. The woman with the hemorrhage came to touch Christ and He took time to minister to her. (See chapter 15.)

Jairus got more and more anxious and afraid as each lingering minute dragged slowly by. His fears were justified. When they finally got near his house, messengers came and said, "Don't bother the Master any more. It's too late. The girl is dead."

It obviously was not said too loudly, but Christ's sympathetic heart and ear overheard the remark (v. 35).

"Don't be afraid!" (v. 36) the Lord said to the father who probably was fighting hard to keep his composure when he realized that all hope was gone. "Only believe!" With these words the Lord was saying, "Look, My friend, don't let your fear destroy your faith. Fear and faith cannot exist beside each other. One pushes the other away. You had enough faith to trust Me that I could heal her when she was at the point of death. Can you now have faith that I can make her whole after she has died?" He then signaled to Peter, James and John and permitted nobody else to go with Him into the house but those three disciples and the child's parents.

The noise, crying, moaning and wailing in the house must have been earsplitting. The richer a man, the more flutes and wailing women were hired. Jairus' household obviously had not spared expenses. "Hush up," Jesus said, "and get out of the house. The girl isn't dead, but asleep" (vv. 38,39).

This antagonized the people and they laughed at His

words and made sarcastic remarks. They knew a dead person when they saw one. They were professionals! They walked out in a huff and assured everyone outside that the girl *was* dead—very dead indeed!

The twelve-year-old girl was still resting on her death bed. In deference to her husband the mother must have waited for Jairus to return before starting preparations for burial.

Jesus again touched a corpse. He took the girl's lifeless, cold hand and said, "*Talitha cumi!*" These are Aramaic words that simply say, "Little teenage girl, I tell you to get up!"

The Bible makes it very clear that Christ again put on no show. He didn't speak in Hebrew or use a famous magic formula. He probably used the same words that Jairus had often used when he woke his little girl up in the morning. Jesus said what a Galilean girl at the age of twelve could understand. So the girl did what she always did when someone woke her up. She jumped out of bed and walked. But she walked a bit wobbly for she might not have eaten for a time.

"You better give her something to eat," Jesus said tenderly. "Healthy twelve-year-olds are always hungry." I can see Him smile while He said it.

"Don't tell anyone what happened," He said before He left. Maybe He didn't want any undue publicity because He knew how upset the Jewish leaders would get if they heard about this second astonishing miracle.

Of course, the story wasn't kept secret. The wailing women had made sure everyone knew that the girl *was* dead, so when she walked out of her house to say "hi" to her crying friends, everyone hurried back home with another exciting story.

The greatest miracle Jesus ever performed happened shortly before His earthly ministry ended. It took place in Judea and started with a great disappointment.

Jesus and the disciples had some very precious friends in Bethany (John 11:1-5), a village nearly two miles from Jerusalem. Lazarus and his sisters, Mary and Martha, had opened their home to the Master and His disciples whenever they needed a place to stay. Jesus did not have a home of His own and depended on friends and their willing hospitality for someplace to rest and relax. The Gospels tell us of a previous visit where the conversation between Jesus and Martha gives us a fine character portrait of the sisters (Luke 10:38-42).

Martha was the impulsive, aggressive, practical woman who ran the home. Most likely she was the older of the two. Mary loved to contemplate and think about the deep things of life, but sometimes she forgot her daily duties in her preoccupation (Luke 10:40). Lazarus was a close friend and very dear to Jesus. This is obvious when we read the message the sisters sent to Jesus when Lazarus suddenly became very ill: "Lord, the one You love is sick" (John 11:3).

They didn't even bother to say: "Hurry and come down to Judea immediately." They were so sure He would come as fast as possible. The disciples thought the same thing. They knew that Jesus loved Lazarus and the two sisters (v. 5).

Jesus and His disciples were on the east side of the Jordan in the region of Perea when the messengers arrived. They worked there to stay away from the Jewish leaders in Jerusalem who tried to capture and kill the Master. The disciples didn't expect anything bad to happen because the Lord had assured them that "Lazarus wasn't sick unto death but his illness would glorify God" (v. 4).

Two days later the Lord said, "Let's go into Judea again" (v. 7).

The disciples argued, "Master, have you forgotten that the Jewish leaders are trying to kill you"(v. 8)?

"No," the Lord answered, "I am aware of it, but I know that nobody can touch Me until My time has come. We need to go and see Lazarus. He is asleep" (v. 11).

The disciples said, "Good, if he sleeps, he is over the crisis."

Christ's favorite description of physical death is "sleep" (Luke 8:52), but the disciples didn't catch on. So, Christ said plainly, "Lazarus is dead."

Thomas, one of Christ's disciples said gloomily, "Let's all go and die together like Lazarus. The thing looks altogether hopeless" (John 11:16).

When they approached Bethany they found that Lazarus had been buried four days before. Martha's and Mary's house was filled with mourners for many Jews from Jerusalem had come to comfort the bereaved sisters. Devout Jews were obligated to such works of love although they didn't come necessarily out of real sympathy but because it was expected of them.

Jesus didn't go to the house. He no doubt tried to avoid the confusion and it was also sensible not to draw the Jew's attention to His return to Judea.

Martha left quietly when she heard of His approach. "Lord," she said, "if You had been here this could not have happened." The Lord answered her with a gentle reproach and tried to teach some spiritual things (John 11:21-17).

Then Martha found Mary and whispered, "The Master has come and He is looking for you" (v. 28).

Mary got up quickly and hurried to find her beloved friend, Jesus. The mourners and visitors followed her because they thought she was going to the new grave.

When Mary saw Jesus she threw herself at His feet and wept. She said exactly the same words Martha had said: "Oh, Lord, if *only* You could have been here" (v. 32).

The Lord didn't answer Mary the same way He did Martha. She received neither a spiritual lecture nor a reminder that He was the great "I AM" (v. 33). He looked at Mary's prostrate form, shaking with deep sobs, and at the rest who had followed her. They cried, too, or at least some of them pretended to show sympathy with a few wails.

"Where is the grave?" the Lord asked and His loving heart ached as He looked at the lot of sinful humanity.

Then He wept (v. 35).

Why did Jesus weep? He already knew that He would raise Lazarus from the dead, so He couldn't have wept in bereavement for His friend. The Bible does not say why Jesus wept but we know that He wept another time when He mourned over Jerusalem (Luke 19:41).

Jesus weeps over unbelief and the slow way people learn. Even His close friends and disciples couldn't grasp it fast enough! Hadn't He raised the young man of Nain and Jairus' daughter? Yes, He had. But the miracles were probably discredited by the Jewish leaders of Judea. After all, a person thought dead might be in a coma or very deep sleep, and Jesus Himself had said the damsel was only asleep.

He heard the mourners say, "Couldn't He have stopped him from dying" (John 11:37)? They sounded so thoughtful and sympathetic, but Christ always knew the motives in the hearts of men. Behind that remark stood an unspoken doubt: obviously there are some things *too hard* for the miracle healer, aren't there? He knows when to come and when to stay away. Even though He loved Lazarus enough to cry over him, He couldn't handle *that* sickness!

Christ groaned as He faced again what He had to face all along. In spite of all the things He had done in nearly three years, people questioned Him as usual. His heart ached to the breaking point.

"Roll away the stone," He commanded.

"Lord," the impulsive Martha said, "do you know what You are doing? It has been four days already and in this heat the body begins to decay and stink very fast."

She again had that slight edge of impatience in her voice, the same tone she used when she said, "*If* You had been here on time, it couldn't have happened."

The Master reproached her again, ever so lovingly: "Martha," He said, "haven't I told you before . . . ? "

Yes, the Lord knew exactly what He was doing. He had known it all along. He didn't even plan it all by Himself. His Father in heaven had it laid out for Him and all He did was wait for exactly the right moment to do His Father's will. Jesus knew that Lazarus would not have died if He had stepped into his room before Lazarus stopped breathing. Death cannot come in contact with the great Life-giver and be victorious. Life in Him was too strong. Christ deliberately stayed away from Lazarus so that Satan could do his dirty work and stop the physical life of His beloved friend.

The Lord stayed away *four* days because ancient Jewish tradition had it that some Jews believed the soul returns for three days to the body in the hope of entering into it again. By the fourth day when the face becomes disfigured, the soul leaves and never returns. For three days the relatives would return to the grave and hope that the person could be in a very deep coma. By the fourth day there remained no doubt that a person was dead. Middle East heat quickly decays a body left above ground.

Christ could have commanded the stone to roll away from Lazarus' tomb by itself, but He never does what human effort can do. And He never gives a show just to impress.

Knowing that the Jewish leaders accused Him of

working together with Satan and doing His miracles by evil power, Christ lifted His eyes to heaven and said confidently, "Father, I thank Thee . . . " (John 11:41).

He made it very clear *who* His Father and His source of power was. Then, He called with a loud voice, "Lazarus come forth!"

Into the stunned silence came a rustle and a shuffle. And Lazarus hobbled out of the cave, bound by his grave clothes.

"Loosen him," the Master said. And again He did not do what humans can do. Christ did what others couldn't do, but He permitted those around Him to be helpers in His great work of mercy.

What a miracle! What a proof of His Messianic authority!

God, the Father, gave the witness three times that Jesus was His life-giving Son and the Saviour of the world. The first two times Satan found a way to cast doubt on the truth of Christ's work, but the third time every smallest avenue of doubt was covered. The man was dead to the point where the flesh began to smell. Enough witnesses from Jerusalem saw the miracle that many believed. However there still were some who didn't want to believe. These took their report to the Pharisees.

As a result the Sanhedrin council met. The chief priests were mostly Sadducees who didn't believe in any life after death. It was irritating and a cause of great embarrassment to try to argue in earnest about such an important doctrine as resurrection while a man like Lazarus walked around Bethany and Jerusalem.

The whole affair had to be brought to an end. On this the Sadducees and Pharisees finally agreed—both Jesus and Lazarus had to die (John 12:9-11).

Wasn't there any way that the Father in heaven could convince His chosen people that the Messiah had arrived and was in their midst to heal and help? No, even God could do only so much, and then He had to let go—reluctantly. God cannot force people to see truth and light because love *never* forces. In the presence of overwhelming proof, people can close their eyes and not see. They did it in Christ's time. They do it today!

Christ's miracle power is still at work. The greatest thing that can *ever* happen is His saving grace which brings people from spiritual death into life that will *never* end.

All three people who were brought back to life by Christ eventually died again. But if they and their families believed in Christ as their Saviour, they received more than another chance to live a few more years—He gave them life eternal (John 3:16).

LET'S PRAY: Dear Lord, great giver of life, I want to thank You that not only do I breathe and live here on earth through Your great love but You gave me eternal life—just for the asking.

I will need all of eternity to be able to grasp such undeserved love more fully, dear God, but I am eager to start learning about it even now.

Because of You I don't have to be afraid of physical death anymore. You told us that our body is only asleep. My born-again spirit shall never die. You'll see to that. Through You I *have* eternal life, not only at a future time but ever since I asked You to come into my heart as my Saviour and Lord.

Why You are so willing to give me life, I shall never know. All I can do is accept and praise You for it, not only on this earth, but forevermore. In Jesus' name always. Amen.

17
JESUS CAME TO MEET HUMAN NEEDS

Public service can be most rewarding but also very tiring, as the disciples discovered after they had been sent out by Jesus to minister to the people. They went out two by two because Jesus knew that two people who work together for God can do a lot more than one person alone (Matthew 18:19). When the disciples returned, they had many stories to tell.

Jesus said, "Let's go to an uninhabited place and rest awhile." He knew human nature so well. Someone who is constantly busy cannot do his best. Rest, relaxation and quiet times with the Lord are essential to effective service.

So they all got into boats and went across the Sea of Galilee to a remote place in the area of Bethsaida Julias (Luke 9:10) which is at the north end of the lake. Things had been so hectic they couldn't even find time to eat. Everybody needed some privacy (Mark 6:32).

But the people noticed their departure and saw the direction in which the boats were going, and they hurried around the lake to the area where the boats most likely would land.

The boats arrived before the people and Jesus went with His disciples into a mountain (or up some hills) to talk and counsel with them. The disciples were pretty upset because Herod had just killed John the Baptist (Mark 6:25-29).

Their rest and sharing time didn't last long because the people quickly caught up with them. What could the loving Master do but welcome them and give them His undivided attention as usual (Mark 6:34). He began to teach them and heal the sick. He kept on teaching and ministering through the entire day. Again, everyone was so involved that they forgot about rest or food. As the sun began to set, the disciples interrupted the Lord in His intense labor of love and said, "Lord, You are forgetting what time it is. You better let the people go. Look where all of us are. There is no place to buy food and the people need to get away before dark (v. 35,36).

Jesus looked into the faces of the disciples and said, "You better give them some food before you send them home" (v. 37).

Philip and Andrew came from the area of Bethsaida and they knew where food could be bought and how much it would cost. They looked over the thousands, milling over the hillside and Philip said, "Lord, You are asking the impossible. Even two hundred penny-worth of food couldn't begin to feed them all" (John 6:7.). Two hundred pennies were two hundred Roman *denarii*. A *denarius* was a whole day's wage for a common laborer or fisherman. Philip actually said, "I would need more that one-half year's income to feed them only meagerly. Lord, be sensible."

Andrew realized that Jesus could not have meant what Philip understood. He looked around to see if *any* food was at hand. And when Jesus asked, "How much food is available?" Andrew had an answer.

"Lord," he said, "there is a young boy here who carried a lunch with him. But it is almost nothing, just five barley loaves and two small fishes. What can that much do for so many" (John 6:9)?

The Bible doesn't tell us the details but I can see Jesus bend down to the young boy and kindly say, "My friend, would you be willing to *give* Me your lunch? I know you are hungry, but I need what you have!"

Jesus would never have taken the boy's food against

his will. The lad, who could not have been thirteen years of age, had been so carried away listening to the Lord's teaching that perhaps he had forgotten to eat at noon time. He handed the little basket with the humble meal to Christ while Jesus told the disciples to seat the people in orderly fashion for a meal. The Greek word indicates that Jesus told the people to recline as this was the custom for eating. While the people put themselves together in groups of fifty or a hundred someone counted the men of the crowd and found five thousand males present (Matthew 14:21).

Women and children were not counted. When the Bible tells us that five thousand men were present, the actual number of people could have been easily ten to fifteen thousand, since many women loved to follow Jesus everywhere (Luke 8:1-3). Women and children were just as important as men were to Jesus. The people sat down on the green grass (John 6:10). The only time the grass in Galilee is green is in winter or spring. This happened just before the Passover Feast (John 6:4), which Bible scholars put in the year A.D. 30.

The Lord had a reason for the orderly seating arrangement. People could neither have been counted nor fed otherwise. Someone could have been overlooked. He also wanted the people to *watch* how He fed them. No doubt He knew that He could later be accused again of foul play by the Jewish leaders. When everyone was seated and all eyes looked at Him, He gave thanks for food which the crowd couldn't see (John 6:11).

Then He broke the five loaves and little fishes into pieces and gave them to the disciples. The Greek word for "gave" means literally "kept on giving"! He never stopped giving and the disciples never stopped handing it out until everybody was full and couldn't eat any more (v. 12).

It wasn't a fancy meal for sure, but it nourished everybody. The flat round barley loaves and dried fishes were simple food, eaten by the poor people of the land. The higher social class of the Jews thought of barley as fodder for animals and a very inferior food. Barley could even be bought in time of famine for far less money than wheat, which was considered superior food (Revelation 6:6).

When everybody, including Jesus and the disciples had his fill, Jesus told the disciples, "Don't let anything go to waste. Go and gather up the leftovers."

The disciples did so and twelve hand baskets were filled with the unused food. Jesus had provided so abundantly that people couldn't eat it all. I am sure that the lad who gave his little meal ended up with a double portion. Young teenagers are hard to fill up and the lad ate his fill until he couldn't get another bite down. He must have felt very pleased with himself that he had been willing to give—look what he got back!

Jesus not only provided that unusual miracle because He understood and had deep compassion for the physical need of the people, but He also knew that hungry people would have a hard time understanding the spiritual things He was teaching. He hadn't forgotten how hunger felt when He fasted for forty days in the wilderness at the beginning of His ministry (Luke 4:2).

In Christ's part of the world eating together was a pledge of friendship. There was nothing that Jesus could have done that would better express to the people that He was their friend. The people got pretty excited about the whole thing. The world looked good after their stomachs were full. And it was easy to accept Jesus as the true prophet (John 6:14,15), or the Messiah. He was the man they had been looking for. His talents could bring not only free bread but what everybody hoped for—the successful revolt against the hated Romans. He could heal wounded soldiers, feed whole armies and even raise the dead. How could the Romans ever beat that? Wasn't it the time to declare Him king immediately? Passover had brought thousands of people to the roads leading to Jerusalem. No doubt many of the crowd with Jesus had been sidetracked on their way to observe the feast in the city of David. They wanted to hear Jesus.

"Let's declare Him king and, if need be, push Him a little," people must have said. "He probably isn't aware how much we are for Him. He needs to be shown" (v. 15).

Jesus knew and He was disturbed. So He sent His disciples to the boats and dismissed the people (Matthew 14:23). Then He found a quiet place to pray. What a temptation Satan set before Jesus under the guise of good intentions of people who wanted "the best" for Him.

It all made such good sense. The disciples were all for it, too. They were tired of being laughed at and accused of following a false prophet. They had given up everything, and for what (Matthew 19:27)? Wasn't it time to put a good show on the road and get things moving in the right direction?

Jesus went to His Father and prayed. His eyes needed to see the spiritual kingdom only—and He no doubt prayed for those who meant so well but couldn't see God's way of doing things (Matthew 14:23).

Meanwhile the disciples were in boats on the lake with the sail set toward Capernaum which was the shortest crossing at that point (John 6:17). The three-and-one-half miles across should not take them more than an hour or two, if the wind was low as it usually is at sunset. They were probably upset again but this time not about John the Baptist's death, but the Master's unreasonable behavior.

Why did He let such a golden opportunity pass to

declare Himself king? Wasn't He thinking of the disciples' position when He made such strange moves, or worse yet, when He didn't make any moves?

I wonder if they noticed that the wind began to blow from the east? East wind always brings trouble for the Sea of Galilee. Suddenly the calm waters began to churn as dark clouds covered the star-studded evening sky. The disciples took to the oars to get to shore, but it was of no avail. They rowed hour after hour, but the wind tossed them toward the midst of the sea (Matthew 14: 24). They were still battling with the storm in the fourth night watch, which was from three to six in the morning (Mark 6:48).

As lightning broke the blackness of the stormy night they saw a figure walking toward them—on top of the angry waves. They thought it was a ghost (spirit) and cried out in terror (Matthew 14:26). Maybe they thought it was the angel of death. The Jews believed strongly that there was an angel of death and they even had a custom of calling a dying person by a different name so the death angel would get confused and look somewhere else for the person he planned to claim.

The disciples didn't switch names or try to fool anybody, they knew they had come to the end. As the figure walked past them they cried out with fear (Mark 6:48, 49). Then Jesus spoke to them and they recognized Him (v. 50).

What a relief!

"Don't be afraid, it is I," Jesus said lovingly. The Greek form of the word means, "I am." Jesus' assurance that the great I Am was with them, again settled their fear. If He would have called Himself the "I was," they would have known that all of them would go under. "I Am" had come to help them.

Jesus had walked for twenty-five to thirty furlongs (John 6:19), which is three miles, to overtake them. He had no other way to get to them because He was tied to His human body.

When He walked on the water He did not use any divine powers that would not be available to another normal human being for the asking. After Peter thought he recognized the Lord, he got a daring idea. "Lord," he said, "if it is really You, let me come to You on the water."

"Come," the Lord said simply (Matthew 14:29). Peter got out of the boat and it worked! He walked on the top of the water (v. 29).

For a moment Peter looked away from the Lord and saw a big wave rolling toward him. It scared brave Peter so badly that he began to sink. "Lord," he screamed, "save me." No doubt the fisherman Peter knew how to swim but in the foaming waters of the raging sea he didn't have a chance. He knew it, too (v. 30)!

The Lord always answers immediately when someone asks Him sincerely for help, be it a real storm or a storm of temptations to a troubled soul. He stretched out His hand and with a secure grip He pulled Peter up and together they climbed into the boat.

After Peter was secure, the Master gave him a loving scolding. "Peter," He said, "why didn't you trust Me more? There was doubt in your heart. Doubt brings fear and when you opened your heart to fear, faith cannot stay. Without faith you couldn't walk on the water, so you began to sink. Peter, will you ever learn to trust Me fully and not doubt My word? (See v. 31.)

As soon as the Lord stepped into the boat, the wind died down (v. 32). The disciples were so overwhelmed by what they had witnessed, they bowed down and worshiped Him as God. They confessed their faith in His divine origin when they said, "Thou art the Son of God."

Nevertheless they were still far away from understanding the true nature of Christ's kingdom. They didn't understand the symbolic meaning of the miracle of the loaves, they did not understand the reason for the storm on the lake for their hearts were hardened (Mark 6:52).

When people are not willing to learn the lessons God so lovingly prepares for them, Jesus has to repeat what He tries to teach. The second time around is always harder.

The disciples had been caught in a terrible storm before (Mark 4:35-41). Circumstances then were similar to this second dreadful night. Everybody was weary from serving the people. Jesus, never using any supernatural power which wasn't available to any other human being, was exhausted. He said, "Let's get into the boats and cross the lake to the other side. We have to get away from the crowd for awhile (v. 35).

The disciples obeyed the Master and He laid down in the boat to sleep while they rowed across. People in other fishing boats eagerly followed (v. 36).

Out of nowhere a great storm arose (v. 37). This is very typical for the Lake of Galilee, even today. Without any warning, without a single cloud in the sky, day or night, a wind can suddenly hit and churn the calm waters within minutes to white foam and fury. Shining stars, a full moon, or bright sunshine may reflect in the angry waves. But mercy on any fishing boat that is out on the water at such a time.

The little boat where Christ rested filled with water and it seemed sure that everybody was lost. The disciples did their best to row and to bail the water out. They were experienced fishermen, but it was of no avail.

Finally they remembered that Jesus was in the boat. They woke Him. They felt rather upset with His ability to sleep through all the uproar and His apparent unconcern. After all, couldn't He get up and help bail out the water which practically covered them" (Matthew 8:24)? At least He could worry a little bit. "Master," they yelled into His ear, "don't You care that we will perish (Mark 4:38)? Please, save us, we are going under" (Matthew 8:25).

I can see what happened next. Jesus stood up in the wobbly boat, calm, unafraid and with complete peace in His entire bearing. He lifted His hand and called out, "Peace, be still." The original meaning of His words actually mean, "Be silent and stay that way!"

The shrieking winds stopped at that same moment and the waters began to calm down. Into the startling silence Jesus said, "How come you are so afraid? Haven't you been with Me long enough to know that you can trust Me? Where is your faith" (Mark 4:40)?

They should have known better. Had they not obeyed the Master's command to cross the sea? Had He not said, "Let's go *to the other side*?" If He said to go to the other side, He meant it. He always means what He says, down to the last little word.

They were deeply impressed by the sudden calmness and were filled with great awe. They asked each other: "What kind of a man is He, that He not only heals the sick, raises the dead but also has power over the elements of nature" (Mark 4:41)? They were always impressed by His miracles but ever so slow to learn what Christ was trying to teach through them.

The Lord seldom did anything outstanding only once. He did most of His great miracles twice or even more times. First of all, He knew that the principles of effective teaching require repetition, at least as far as we human beings are concerned. Second, He knew that He needed witnesses in His favor. One of the rules which He Himself had given Israel in the wilderness, before He took on a human form, was, "Don't condemn anyone by *one* witness alone. There must be two or three witnesses" (Deuteronomy 19:15; Matthew 18:16). He knew that the Jews would condemn Him, but He made sure that they did it in the presence of those who had witnessed His work and could not be disproved.

No doubt when the story was told of the first time He calmed the sea, His enemies said, "It was pure coincidence. The storms on the lake often stop as suddenly as they start." Maybe some of His disciples had begun to wonder if it really had been as spectacular as they remembered it.

However, the second time there was no room for doubt. Everybody knew that He could master a storm. He could even walk on the tops of angry waves.

Jesus also repeated the feeding of a multitude of people. It happened when He returned from His trip to Canaan where He had healed the daughter of the Syrophoenician woman.

The Bible does not give us the exact location where the second crowd gathered. It was another mountain near the Sea of Galilee where multitudes came to Him and brought the sick to be healed (Matthew 15:29-31). Bible scholars believe that the area was near Gergesa, which would be on the east side of the lake.

This incident appears similar to the feeding of the five thousand, but we find enough marked differences that we know there were two different occasions.

The crowd stayed longer this time—for three days (Mark 8:2). During this time they watched the dumb speak, the lame walk, the blind see and the maimed become whole. People who had lost a limb or part of their body grew a new part and were suddenly normal and complete. The people watched and they glorified the God of *Israel* (Matthew 15:31). The first time, the people were on the way to the Passover; they were devout Jews. This time the people praised and acknowledged the God of Israel, which tells us that among the second crowd were many Gentiles. Maybe they had followed Jesus when He left the heathen land from which He had just returned. Many had come a great distance (Mark 8:3).

People may have had food with them earlier for nobody suggested that there was a problem until Christ spoke up. He said to His disciples, "I feel sorry for the people. They ran out of provisions and it's a long way home for them. They will faint in the heat of the desert and die before they get out of the wilderness."

The disciples answered, "How can we find that much bread in the wilderness to feed so many people?" Had the disciples already forgotten how the last crowd had been fed just a few weeks or months earlier? It does not sound reasonable, does it? Why would they suggest that the people be sent away hungry? Because they couldn't believe that Jesus would perform a miracle for a mixed multitude of mostly heathen. Had He not Himself said, "Bread is for the children only" (Mark 7:27)? They had forgotten that He *did* give the bread to the heathen woman as an answer to her faith and an object lesson to the disciples. The disciples were very slow to learn (Matthew 15:15,16; 16:9-11).

The Lord said, "How much food is available?"

The disciples found seven loaves and a few little fish. We do not know what kind of bread they found this time, but the original meaning of the word simply suggests leavened bread of any kind.

He repeated His mission of mercy and the disciples asked the people to sit down. No green grass this time, the sun had burned the desert brown. The men were counted again and there were four thousand present, besides women and children.

After the people had eaten, the unused food was again gathered up. It filled seven large baskets, the type of baskets people would carry with them when they went on a long journey. The first time twelve hand baskets were filled.

I am sure that the people took the leftover food home with them to share with others. It was "blessed" and very special, wasn't it?

The comparison of the numbers in these two miracles has always intrigued me. Human arithmetic would conclude that if Jesus used five loaves for five thousand people and ended up with twelve baskets, He would use four loaves for four thousand people and have nine or ten baskets left over. God's arithmetic does not follow human reasoning. He used more food the second time for less people and ended up with a different amount left over. What was it that Christ tried to show with these two similar miracles?

First of all, He respected and had deep compassion for the physical needs of *all* people, not only the Jews. Next, He showed that He, the bread of life, would have to be broken to all nations, although it was to begin with His own chosen people (John 6:51; Romans 1:16). I am sure that His disciples remembered all those things later when Jesus left them to go back to His Father.

The unmatching arithmetic tells us that Christ did not work by cut-and-dried formulas. He can take whatever is available, even that which is simple and inferior in the eyes of men, and bless and multiply it for the good of the masses. As long as He has something or somebody to work with, and all is *given* to Him, He can use it.

If we wonder how the disciples could have been so slow to learn in the presence of His overwhelming miracles, are we truly that much better? How often do we lift our eyes over the millions of the world and say, "How shall the gospel ever be preached to all the world? How can we break the bread of life to *every* nation? We have so little!"

It does not matter how few and small our loaves are

which we bring to Jesus. It does not matter that we have nothing fancy to offer. The only thing that matters is that we give Him *all* that we have. He will do the rest.

LET'S PRAY: Dear Jesus, I always wished I could have been the person who gave the bread and the fishes for You to use. I keep forgetting that I *do* have bread in my hand and house, not only physical food but the bread of life for a hungry world. I want to give it to You, all of it! Please, bless it and multiply it and make me the disciple who hands it out. I do the running but You do the miracle and all the honor and the glory must always go to You alone. Amen.

18
JESUS CAME TO CLEANSE AND DRIVE OUT DEMONS

Of all the sicknesses in Christ's time, leprosy was the most feared and dreaded. It was considered an incurable disease. A leper suffered not only disfigurement and an agonizing slow death, but also separation from family and friends and total isolation, except from other lepers. A leper was declared unclean by Mosaic law and had to move out of his community into uninhabited areas. If a leper came near a village he was required to ring a little bell, and when he saw anyone approaching him, he was supposed to warn the person by calling out, "Unclean, unclean" (Leviticus 13:45).

Nobody was allowed to touch a leper or anything he had touched or else that person became unclean for at least one day (Leviticus 13—14). The leper was punished severely if he came in contact with anyone else.

Leprosy was considered more than just a sickness. It was interpreted as a divine punishment for immorality and sin. Therefore the Bible writers did not speak of "healing" lepers, but they were "cleansed" of sin and their outward evidence of it.

Three of the Gospels record a time when Jesus cleansed a leper; it must have been important to the writers (Matthew 8:2-4; Mark 1:40-44; Luke 5:12-14).

One desperate leper broke the social code while Jesus was preaching and healing on His first tour through Galilee. He broke through the crowd and fell at Jesus' feet. Humbly, he said, "*If* Thou wilt, Thou canst make me clean" (Mark 1:40).

The poor leper had reasons to say, "If You *want* to do it, You can." He couldn't be sure that Jesus would do it. Maybe the Lord also thought that the leper had come under God's disfavor and abandonment, just as everyone else did. The Bible doesn't record any incidence of a leper being cleansed since Elisha did it, nearly one thousand years before.

The people must have moved away in panic when they saw that a leper had entered the group. Jesus didn't. He reached out and *touched* Him. Ever so kindly and lovingly He said, "I *will*, be thou clean" (v. 41).

The same moment the man's skin changed. The white oozing spots disappeared; flesh and muscles grew back and the man appeared healthy and normal. No doubt the man bubbled over with joy, but Jesus told him rather sternly not to talk about it.

"Go to the priest and have yourself checked over and do what is required of you by the Law," the Lord said (v. 44). A cleansed leper had to go through various ceremonies to be declared clean by the authorities. It took a whole week to accomplish it all (Leviticus 14).

Jesus may have been concerned that if the leper told *how* he had been cured the priests would not have been willing to give him a clean bill of health. Also, if the story of the healing spread, many lepers would come only for the sake of healing, not to be taught and helped spiritually. Jesus shied away from spectacular shows and did any miracle only to meet a genuine human need, not to impress the crowds.

The leper didn't obey Jesus too well; he told his story to everybody. It was simply too good to be true and he couldn't help but announce it everywhere he went (Mark 1:45). As a result, people came in such big numbers that the Lord couldn't show Himself publicly for a while but had to go into seclusion. Even there the people found Him as they came from all around the country.

The story of the cleansed leper must have made the rounds among many lepers in the northern area.

When Jesus crossed through Samaria and Galilee *ten* lepers approached the famous healer as He was about to enter a village (Luke 17:12-19). They stood afar off as the law required (v. 12) and called in a loud voice for help and mercy (v. 13).

Jesus never had any "set" pattern of healing. This time He didn't touch them but just gave them a short command. "Go and show yourselves to the priest," He said (v. 14). However it wasn't until they obeyed and were on their way that the leprosy left them. By an act of their faith they were healed. Obedience and faith go hand in hand. Even though all ten men were healed, only one returned to thank Jesus.

Jesus made it clear that God deserved words of praise. He asked where the nine healed Jews were. The one grateful fellow who came back to show his gratitude was a despised foreigner from Samaria (vv. 15,16). How could the nine lepers have been so thoughtless as to forget to thank the kind Master?

How is it that so many people who have been cleansed of their sins forget to thank their Saviour and gripe, murmur and complain? Which is the greater miracle: the cleansing of a diseased body or the cleansing of a sin-sick, poisoned soul? Jesus not only healed visible diseases; He also forgave sins (Mark 2:5).

One of my favorite stories is recorded by John. While Jesus sat in the Temple and taught, (something He loved to do more than spectacular healing) the scribes and Pharisees brought a woman to Him caught in the act of adultery (John 8:3). They said to Him, ever so sanctimoniously, "Master (Teacher), what do *You* suggest we should do?"

It was clearly a trap and everybody knew it. Jesus acted as if He didn't hear them. He stooped down and began writing in the sand. Finally He said, "He who is without sin, let him cast the first stone" (v. 7).

He then kept on writing and one by one the accusers left, convicted by their own conscience (v. 9).

What happened? Some have suggested that Jesus wrote down the sins of the woman's prosecutors. If He did, Jesus handled the situation beautifully. He was tactful. He didn't tell on the men in front of each other. Temple traffic would erase His writings and not embarrass the leaders. Nevertheless He let it be known very clearly that He was aware of their own shortcomings.

Quietly the eldest, most respected man left. He wasn't too eager to have his private life made public. One by one they disappeared, the youngest and least in importance got his record last and he finally left also.

Jesus looked up, "Woman," He said, "is anybody left to accuse you?"

"No," the trembling woman said, "they are all gone."

"I don't condemn you either," Jesus said kindly. "Go and sin *no more!*"

Two or three witnesses would have been needed to condemn the adulterous woman. Since Christ was the only one left and no accuser was present, He could and would not proclaim judgment on her.

Does that mean that Christ overlooks sin? No, He does not! Christ didn't come to condemn but to save the world (John 3:17). He disapproved of sin in every form. He did not declare one sin worse than another. Adultery is wrong (Matthew 5:27,28) but so is self-righteousness and judging. The men were as wrong as was the immoral woman. Everybody needed forgiveness and cleansing by the Saviour of the world. The proud men never repented of their sins, at least, the Bible gives no record of it.

Did the woman who was pardoned and sent away by Christ ever change? The Bible does not say so, but some

Bible scholars believe that the adulterous woman was Mary Magdalene, out of whom Jesus drove seven devils (Mark 16:9). I like to believe that the woman became an ardent follower of the Lord. His kindness and love must have overwhelmed this one who tried to fulfill her human needs the wrong way. When she found true love she accepted it. Love covers a multitude of sin (1 Peter 4:8).

If the sinful woman was the one who had seven demons cast out of her, she needed to be pitied, not stoned. Demon possession is a dreadful thing. At the time of Christ many people were possessed by unclean and evil spirits, so much so that the New Testament emphasized the fact that Christ came to cast out demons (Mark 1:34). He in turn sent His disciples out with authority over the Satanic spirits (Mark 3:15).

We find a great many stories about the casting out of evil spirits who controlled human beings. Satan loves to get in control of a human being. The stories don't tell us how the people got themselves under that power, but we know how they were delivered.

The Gospels give six narratives about demon possession (Matthew 9:32-34; 15:21-28; Mark 1:21-28; 5:1-20; 9:14-29; 16:9). In addition to these specific stories, the Gospels often mention that Jesus and His disciples healed those tormented and possessed by evil spirits (Luke 4:40,41; 7:21; 9:1; 10:17).

A man with an unclean spirit interrupted the Lord while He taught at the synagogue in Capernaum (Mark 1:23-28). "What have we to do with Thee, Thou Jesus of Nazareth," cried the demon.

"Jesus of Nazareth" was a term of disrespect and a put-down. Christ never called Himself that name. His enemies called Him such, to show that He had no decent family name and came from a place of ill repute (John 1:46). Satan and his demons delighted to call Jesus an ugly name but they had to admit that He *was* the Holy One of Israel. Even though Satan acknowledged that Jesus was the Son of God, he also antagonized the Jewish leaders to wrath when Christ claimed His divinity.

Christ understood Satan's foul play and He rebuked him by saying "Hold thy peace and come out of the man." "Hold thy peace" means in its original meaning, "be muzzled" or "be and remain still," the same word Christ used to still the storm at sea.

The evil spirit "tore" the poor victim. He attacked him, trying most likely to destroy him, but in the presence of the lifegiver, Satan could not kill. In Christ, Satan's spirits had found a new authority. The demons knew it and so did the people (Mark 1:26,27).

Christ used neither magic formula, incantations, charms or chants to exhort the spirits. He needed no superstitious procedures. Jesus gave a simple command and the demons fled.

That was more than obvious when Jesus faced the two demoniacs of Gadara (Matthew 8:28). One of them must have been vicious because Mark and Luke tell of one who cried out and ran toward the Lord (Mark 5:7; Luke 8:28). Instead of attacking Him, the man threw himself down and worshiped Jesus. Jesus commanded the unclean spirit to come out of the man. Then He asked the spirit for his name. The possessed man did not speak but the demons used his voice to reply to Jesus: "Legion, for we are many" (Luke 8:30). Then they pleaded with Jesus not to destroy them (v. 31).

A legion consisted of six thousand troops. Could one human being be filled with that many evil spirits? Whatever it indicated, enough evil power was in one or two human beings that when driven out, the evil spirits were able to destroy a whole herd of swine (v. 33).

Christ never underestimated the vicious power of Satan and his evil spirits, but people do! They think they can take demons on by themselves.

The disciples found out the power of demons when they tried to cast one out of a young boy who had been brought to them by his father. Jesus and His three special companions had been up on the Mount of Transfiguration and came down, talking about spiritual things. They found the other nine disciples surrounded by a multitude of people and amidst great commotion (Mark 9:14).

The disciples had tried to free the possessed boy of the demon and it didn't work. They were embarrassed and puzzled. After all they had done it with success before (Mark 6:7,13).

Christ questioned the father who told Him a sad, agonizing story about the torture the child had gone through for so long. He then said to Jesus *"If* You can do *any* thing, please help us" (Mark 9:22). The man felt justified to question Christ's power. After all had not the Master's disciples failed?

Jesus knew that if He even failed *once*, He would lose His messianic claim. Christ never did anything in His own power. He always worked through His Father's power (Mark 9:23-27; John 5:36). Satan also knew that if Christ failed one time His authority would be gone. So he tried to cast blame on Christ for His disciples' failure. But the disciples had not failed. The father's "if" showed where the failure was—in the man's own unbelief. Christ put the problem where it belonged. He said, "If *you* can believe, all things are possible to him that believes."

The father saw his own great mistake and said with tears, "Lord, I want to believe, please help me and take the unbelief away" (Mark 9:24).

Jesus commanded the evil spirit to get out and not to return. The demon obeyed but again tried to kill the boy before it left (v. 26). He couldn't! The grateful father took a normal healthy boy home and the disciples felt rather foolish.

"Lord," they said, "why couldn't *we* cast him out?" (Mark 9:28).

The Lord said, "This violent evil type of a spirit obeys only people who are in an attitude of prayer and fasting" (Mark 9:29; Matthew 17:21). With that He said, "Look, you got a bit too sure of yourself and didn't depend fully on the power of God. If there is anything in you that separates you from the Father in heaven, you are in for defeat. When you fail, you not only end up embarrassed for yourself, but you bring shame on *My* name. Just as I never do anything without My Father, so you better do nothing without Me (John 15:5). I have the authority over Satan, you don't! So you better face evil always in *My* name, not by yourself. If you do that, you don't need a fancy ceremony. It takes nothing but a simple command and Satan will flee!"

The disciples didn't understand what He said. Not then! They also didn't understand that evil spirits could come into a human heart without great noise and crazy demonstrations.

No doubt the respected leaders of the Jewish nation carried evil spirits in them as they plotted to kill Jesus. Among the twelve disciples walked one who already carried Satan's spirit in himself. Satan's unclean spirits will always try to enter into people, even the souls of Christ's followers.

No human being is able to drive out such supernatural forces in others or in themselves unless they do it Christ's way. And Christ said that it is an attitude of prayer and fasting that brings us in line with the power and authority of the Holy One, Jesus Christ. Before Him, the demons tremble (James 2:19).

There is as much demon possession in the world today as there was in Christ's time. What are we doing about it? Are we doomed to fail as His disciples did, or do we have the same authority Jesus had? The choice is with us. *If* we believe . . . *all* things are possible to him that believes *in Jesus*" (John 14:11-13).

LET'S PRAY: Dear Jesus, You are not only my Lord, but my Master over the demons. Help me to remember that I *never* have to be afraid of Satan and his evil spirits as long as I am covered by Your blood.

I am asking You, precious Lord, to put me under Your power and in Your name, dear Jesus, I *command* the evil spirits to leave. Satan, you are rebuked and bound and under the authority of the Son of God. So you must go away. You can never destroy me and I can demand that you stop annoying me. I belong to Jesus alone. You demons cannot stay, but go to the place God has reserved for you! In Jesus' holy and powerful name. Amen.

19
THE FATHER GLORIFIES HIS SON

Things had not gone too well for the Lord in quite a while. Jesus' archenemies the Pharisees and Sadducees were determined to silence Him for good. The Lord and the disciples even had to leave the northern area of Galilee once in awhile to get away from the Jews' antagonism (John 10:39,40). The moment Christ returned to Galilee, they hunted Him again.

"Give us a special sign from heaven," they repeatedly demanded. "If You do that, we might believe in You" (Matthew 16:1).

Christ knew they didn't believe in the presence of the clear evidence they already had. So why would they believe if He put a special show on? He never did any miracle except to meet a genuine human need. He also never broke any natural laws. He only applied a higher law or contracted time to bring an instant result.

A person who is healed in a month or a year is healed by the same miracle power that touched the person whom Christ made whole in a moment. The same power that grew a grain of wheat in stages out of *one* seed (Mark 4:27,28), multiplied the bread that fed the hungry multitude.

The Jews could have seen the sign if they wanted to. The Lord tried to reason with them but to no avail (Matthew 16:2-4). He never argued for the sake of arguing. So He left them and went by boat across the lake. Then, Jesus and His disciples walked about twenty-five miles north until they got into the vicinity of Caesarea Philippi, a Roman border town within Galilee (Matthew 16:13-16). In that area is a famous rock which in ancient times, was dedicated to the Greek god Pan, the patron god of shepherds and hunters. Out of the cliff springs a perennial stream, one of the chief sources of the Jordan River. The water seems to appear from nowhere and the heathen worshiped at this place where the gods brought forth never-ending water.

Tradition places Peter's confession of faith at the moment when Jesus and the disciples stood below the towering cliff and perhaps drank from the crystal clear spring water.

Jesus began to question His disciples, "Whom do men say that I, the Son of Man, am" (Matthew 16:15)? The term "Son of Man" was often used by Jesus to describe Himself. It was an Old Testament term that described a prophet, one who spoke in behalf of God. Ezekiel uses the term more than ninety times (Ezekiel 2:1-4; see also Matthew 16:27,28; Mark 2:10).

The disciples told Jesus the different ideas various people had (Matthew 16:14).

Jesus then turned to them and said, "And who do *you* think and say that I am" (v. 15)?

Peter often seemed to be the spokesman of the group. He said, "Thou art the Christ, the Son of the living God" (v. 16). Peter's answer was a declaration of faith and loyalty at a time when the people began to turn against Jesus. Many followers had already left Him (John 6:66). The disciples were slow to learn but they did cling to their conviction that Jesus was the Christ.

Jesus said, "Blessed are you, Simon bar-Jona!" He called him by his full Jewish family name, Simon, son of Jonah or John. Then He continued, "Human understanding could not have given you such great revelation. You got this statement straight from My Father, the

God of heaven" (Matthew 16:17). "You are Peter." Now Jesus switched names and He called Peter by the name He had given him when they met for the first time (John 1:42). The original form of the name is *petros* which means a small, movable stone or pebble. "Upon *this* rock I will build my church," Christ said solemnly (Matthew 16:18).

Some people and Bible scholars claim that Christ built His church on Peter and appointed him at that moment to be the head of the first Christian church. The Catholic Church uses the text to make Peter the first pope. But the Lord did not say, "I build My church on *petros* (a moving, unstable little rock)." The original word gives us the word, *petra* which means a big, solid ledge, a living rock that has never been moved out of the original position. Christ refers to the same kind of rock in His parable of the wise man who built his house on a *petra* (Matthew 7:24).

When Christ said, "I build My church on *this* rock," He for sure didn't point at Peter or the famous rock that had been dedicated to Pan. He pointed to Himself!

"Look, little stone," He said, "you are part of the future construction of which *I am* the foundation. Don't trust any other rock, not even the sacred Jewish rock in the Temple in Jerusalem where the lambs are slain. I Myself will build My church and the gates of hell will not hold up against it. The church will advance and triumph" (Matthew 16:18).

No doubt Christ looked ahead and saw His church—feeble, imperfect, persecuted, lukewarm and always attacked by Satan down through the ages. But because He builds the church on Himself and not on human beings, she will triumph, just as He would triumph at the time when everything would look most hopeless on Golgotha. His church will, like Christ, be the strongest and will break the gates of hell when it appears to be defeated.

Peter was not the foundation of the church but he and the other disciples carried the keys to open the doors of the Christian church to others. They had been taught by Jesus Himself for years and Christ's teachings had to be opened up to the rest of the world after Jesus had gone (Matthew 28:18-20).

The disciples did not see Christ's statement as a promotion of Peter as their leader. This is obvious when we read later on that they argued repeatedly about who was the greatest among them (Matthew 18:1; Luke 9:46). Just in case Peter did see himself a bit better than the rest, the Lord had a remarkable way of keeping the fisherman humble. Peter had a fast tongue and was slow to learn. The Lord had to keep him in his place.

After the disciples' declaration Jesus tried to open their understanding to the things right ahead of Him. He attempted to prepare them for the great shock and disappointment when they would see Him not on an earthly throne of David but on a despised cross (Matthew 16:21). Peter decided to straighten the Master out. He took Him aside for a private talk and said, "Stop that terrible talk about dying! You are the Messiah and You are on the road to fame and honor—and so are we, your loyal disciples" (Matthew 16:22).

Christ didn't permit Peter to go on with his well-meant sweet talk. He said, "Peter, you, who just had a great revelation from My Father, are being used by Satan right now. May Satan in you get lost" (v. 23). Christ used the same words to stop Peter He had used to end Satan's temptation in the wilderness (Matthew 4:10).

What a lesson! The same person to whom God entrusts great revelations may be used by Satan as soon as pride and unwillingness to accept Christ's way enters his heart.

The Lord didn't keep a grudge against Peter, though.

He saw the sincerity of his heart and knew that someday he would learn, although it would have to be the hard way!

A week later we find Jesus and His three special companions, John, James and Peter, climbing a high mountain (Matthew 17:1). Tradition claims it to be Mount Tabor. Some Bible scholars suggest Mount Hermon. Nobody knows for sure which mountain it was, but we do know what happened on top of a mountain. Jesus was transfigured before the eyes of His three disciples. The word in Greek, *metamorphoomai*, is the word from which we get "metamorphosis" and means to "change into another form." Jesus changed His appearance while He prayed. His Father surrounded Him with heavenly glory and everything about Jesus shone (v. 2).

The disciples slept while Jesus prayed and when they awoke they found the sparkling transfigured form of Jesus talking with two heavenly visitors: Moses and Elijah. Peter had a great talent of speaking up when silence would have been golden. He said, "Lord, let's stay up here. We'll make a booth for all three of you—Elijah, Moses and You" (v. 4).

Why Peter suggested it is not known. We find many speculations about it. All we know is that Peter's eagerness to "do something" was applied at the wrong time and place. He wasn't in charge. God was!

A bright cloud lit up the sky and a voice said, "This is My beloved Son, listen to *Him*" (v. 5)! Even God in heaven tried to open the disciples' understanding. The Father actually said: "You are right, He *is* My Son. So you'd better be still and listen. You are doing too much talking. You always want to keep busy with earthly things. My Son has the real answer. Just listen!"

The heavenly visitors left and the cloud faded. Peter and the disciples fell on their faces in fear; they had nothing more to say. Jesus touched them. What a thoughtful, kind friend He was. He said, "Don't be afraid." The disciples looked up and saw Jesus *alone* (v. 7,8). How good it would have been if the three disciples had remained in that state. To always see Jesus alone would keep many temptations and mistakes away. But they went down the mountain and saw again too many earthly things to distract them from keeping their eyes only on Jesus.

The first time the Father spoke and honored His Son was at Christ's baptism when He pronounced His blessing on Christ's ministry (Matthew 3:17). The second time God's voice told the three disciples, "Whatever He says, *listen* to it."

The Father sent His voice from heaven once more at the end of Christ's earthly ministry. Jesus had visited the Temple perhaps for the last time. He did what He enjoyed most: He taught the people. He usually taught while sitting in the Court of the Women, which was also the treasury. Only Jews were allowed in the place. While Jesus was there the disciples mingled with the crowd in the outer court. Some Greeks came up to Philip and said, "Sir, we would love to see Jesus" (John 12:21).

Philip didn't know how to handle the situation. After all the Greeks were Gentiles and couldn't go into the treasury. Should he go in and interrupt Jesus' teaching for the sake of some foreigners? He decided to ask Andrew. Andrew seemed to know better what to do. He was more practical and able to understand what Jesus would want them to do. Andrew and Philip decided to walk in and inform Jesus about His visitors from a western country. When Jesus heard the news His face must have lit up with joy. "The time has come when the Son of man should be glorified," He said (John 12:23).

Jesus responded to the request of a few strangers so warmly because His human heart was encouraged by the Greeks' desire to see Him. Christ stood at the brink of human disaster and a horrible death. The Jews rejected Him, the disciples refused to follow His thinking and were unable to grasp His teaching and by human evaluation His life and ministry were a total failure.

The Father lovingly sent the Greeks to remind Christ that He could look toward a harvest of souls all over the world. The Greeks were only a symbol of the people down through the ages who would come and say, "We would see Jesus."

But before the harvest a kernel of grain must fall into the ground and disintegrate before it can grow more grain (John 12:24). Until it does so, the seed remains alone. Christ knew that between Him and a great harvest stood a cross. His human nature felt troubled when He contemplated the suffering just ahead of Him. But He knew that He had come to this earth for this hour of suffering—and to glorify His Father's name (vv. 27, 28).

Jesus had done His best every moment of His life. He could do no more! Now the Father had to glorify His name. Christ's work was about to be finished. Jesus prayed, "Father, glorify Your name" (v. 28). By it He said, "Reveal Your character and show Your nature and personality." For the name in Jewish time typified a person's whole being.

The Father answered, "I have both glorified it, and will glorify it again" (v. 28). With this the Father said, "I glorified it in the past, and I'll glorify it again—in the death and resurrection of Him Whom you reject."

The people listened and some said, "An angel has spoken." Others said, "It thundered" (v. 29). How typical of people who come to a place of worship. Some hear only noise, others the voice of God. To hear God a person must not only listen with the ears but also with the heart. So often people nullify what God has glorified!

LET'S PRAY: Dear Father in heaven, I long to glorify Your name as Your Son Jesus did. So often what I try to do for You looks like a total failure. But why should I be treated differently than they treated my Lord? He gave everything and they only made fun of it. I thank You that You often send incidents that encourage me when I am ready to give up.

Whenever I think my labor for souls is completely in vain, You let me know that only eternity will reveal what has been done. My blundering attempts might look different in the glory of Your kingdom. I just have to trust You as Jesus did.

I'm asking You to glorify Your name through my clumsy, faltering attempts to bring people to Jesus. As I lift up His name, He will draw the people unto Himself. I don't have to and I am glad. I am no more than Philip was, but it's enough to gladden Jesus' heart, and Yours. Amen.

20
HOSANNA TO THE SON OF DAVID

The Passover feast of the Jews always comes in early spring when spring rains have brought flowers, green grass and new leaves to the trees (Song of Solomon 2:11-13).

Jesus and His disciples arrived in Bethany six days before the Passover ceremonies began. No doubt they all stayed with Lazarus, Martha and Mary (John 12:1).

After the sunset of the Sabbath day, Simon, the one Christ had healed of leprosy, gave a dinner in His honor (Mark 14:3). It is possible that this Simon is the same man who also was a Pharisee and who had given a meal in Jesus' honor before (Luke 7:36-40).

At the first dinner a woman of sin had come to Simon's house and anointed the Lord's feet with tears and expensive ointment (v. 38). One wonders if she was the grateful woman Jesus had sent home uncondemned when she was caught in the act of adultery (John 8:10, 11)?

Simon not only invited Jesus and the disciples, but also Lazarus and his sisters, Martha and Mary. While people ate, Mary did the same thing the sinful woman did, she anointed the Master's head and feet. She did not have to crawl under the table to do so, because in the more well-to-do Jewish homes during Christ's time people reclined on couches or cushions to eat. They took their sandals off as they entered a house. When they reclined on the cushions, they leaned on their left arm while they ate with their right hand. The left arm rested near the table and the feet were at the lower end of the couch, away from the table. The tables were arranged in U-form so that food could be brought through the open end and served from the inner U-side only. Therefore it was relatively simple for Mary to get to Christ's feet. To kiss and embrace someone's feet was most appropriate and a sign of highest regard.

I have always believed the two women in the two narratives were the same Mary (Mary Magdalene and Mary of Bethany) with her name simply being changed when she returned to a respectable life (see Luke 7:37, 38 and John 12:1-8). The thing that gives it away to me is that Mary used her hair to wipe the Master's feet. She did that before when she washed His feet with her tears (Luke 7:37,38). A respectable woman would *never* let her hair down in public before the eyes of strangers. She had to use a head covering that hid every bit of hair. A woman of sin, a prostitute, didn't hide her hair. She used it to entice men. When the sinful woman let her hair down, Simon thought, "Why isn't Jesus aware of the type woman she is?" Out of the incident a most interesting conversation developed (Luke 7:39-50).

Now we find the respectable Mary of Bethany doing the same thing. When she did it the second time, she tried to do it very quietly. She knew she would be in trouble with her proper sister Martha for doing such an improper thing! (Her behavior was enough of a shocker that the Gospel writer mentions it.)

Why did she do it? Was she telling Jesus, "I haven't forgotten what You did for me; I know it was You who pulled me out of the pit. I'll be Your loyal follower forever, regardless of what others say about You or me!"

But the scent of the perfume gave her away. Judas Iscariot, one of Christ's disciples spoke up, maybe under his breath. "What a terrible waste," he said. "The perfume could have been sold for a fortune, at least $6,000, and the money given to the poor" (John 12:4,5).

Judas had no business worrying about it. He was the one who carried the common purse and often had his long fingers in it to steal from the others (v. 6). Judas kept everybody so short that Jesus even had to perform a miracle to pay His and Peter's taxes to Rome (Matthew 17:24-27). Fancy being worried about the poor! How often people try to cover up their own sins by criticizing others!

Jesus looked at the disciples and said, "Leave her alone! She is preparing Me for My burial. You can help the poor for a long time to come but I am with you only a little while longer. She did the best she knows how, isn't that enough? Her loving act will be told down the ages and people will know why she did it" (Mark 14:9).

Judas got rather unhappy because Christ had taken the side of a *woman* against him and his statement. Soon he left the party and had a secret meeting with the Jewish leaders of Jerusalem (v. 10).

The Lord's defense of Mary made Judas more determined than ever to manipulate Jesus into doing what the disciples wanted Him to do: declare Himself king of the Jews. All the strange talk about death and burial bothered everybody, but Judas decided to do something drastic about it. He had a meeting with the chief priests of Israel because they had announced that anyone seeing Jesus must report Him immediately so that they could arrest Him (John 11:53-57).

The Bible does not say so, but I believe that Judas had a special scheme in his sharp mind. He knew that Jesus had great power to deliver people from anything that was evil. He figured that Jesus would be forced to act and begin a revolution against the chief leaders and the Romans if they laid hands on Him. He would for once deliver Himself and not others and by this make the move everybody waited for: declare Himself as the promised Messiah and rightful heir to the throne of David (Luke 1:32,33).

Jesus did declare Himself king but in a different way than people anticipated it.

The next morning, which was Sunday morning, He told two of His disciples to go to the next village above Bethany. Bethany lies at the eastern slopes of the Mount of Olives. The village close to the rest of the eastern side of the mountain is Bethphage which means in Aramaic, "house of unripe figs."

The Lord said, "Go to that village and you will find a donkey and a colt on which no one has ever ridden (Matthew 21:2; Mark 11:2). Bring it to me! If anyone asks you what you are doing, just say, 'The Master needs the animal' " (Mark 11:3).

The disciples obeyed and found the ass and the young colt tied up by a housegate in the street (v. 4). Most oriental dwellings of Christ's time (even up to the present time) had an inner courtyard and a passageway leading out to the street. Animals were usually tethered in the courtyard, not at the outer gate.

When the disciples untied the lowly animal, the owner asked: "What are you doing?"

The disciples replied, "The Lord needs him" (Luke 19:33,34). Nothing more needed to be said. Everybody got the message without further explanation: Jesus was *finally* asking for a colt. He was at last doing what they had been waiting for!

Ever since King Solomon every Jewish king rode to his coronation on a young donkey (1 King 1:38). Solomon chose to do so because his father David had been a man of war and he wanted to show that he was a king of peace. Horses were animals that symbolized war but donkeys were never used to draw a war chariot (1 Samuel 13:5).

The prophet Zechariah had foretold that the Messiah

would enter the city of David on a lowly donkey (Zechariah 9:9).

The disciples' hearts must have overflowed with excitement and they probably told everyone the electrifying news. Jesus, who had shunned publicity and special displays as long as they knew Him, had at last changed His mind. The hour of triumph and victory had come! Israel's shame would soon be over. The Romans would shortly be expelled and the earthly kingdom of David and Solomon restored. They brought the young animal to the Master and threw some of their clothing across its back (Mark 11:7).

Every former Jewish king had fancy covers on his animal, special clothing on himself and rode through streets decorated and laid out with flowers, branches and soft ground covers. Jesus had asked for no special decoration but the disciples and His many friends did their best to make it a royal procession anyway.

No doubt He started out with a crowd of people because so many had come to Bethany to see not only Him but also Lazarus who had returned from the grave. (The story of his rising from the dead had spread so far and wide and made Jesus so popular that Jewish leaders decided to kill Lazarus also, John 12:9,10.)

As the procession progressed more and more people joined the throng. The Bible does not tell us who all were in the multitudes, but we can be sure that Lazarus and the two sisters were in it, perhaps many who had been healed and helped by Him, and of course, many, many curious bystanders who got caught up in the excitement. Up the eastern slope of the mountain moved the crowd and when they got to the top, Jerusalem lay below them, across the narrow Kidron Valley. It was the custom for pilgrims who came to Jerusalem for a religious feast to break out in song when they caught the first glimpse of the city. Usually they sang psalms like

Psalms 121 and 122 which were called the psalms of the ascents.

As Jesus rode slowly down the western slope of the Mount of Olives, the people shouted Old Testament passages and sang, "Hosanna to the Son of David. Blessed is He that cometh in the name of the Lord" (Mark 11:9-11; Psalm 118:26). They not only spread their garments before the Lord as a customary sign of homage to His royalty (2 Kings 9:13), but they also broke off branches from the olive trees which covered the Mount of Olives. They climbed the palm trees and broke off palm branches and waved them. What excitement and fun it was for everyone—except for Jesus. As He neared Jerusalem, He stopped. His strong masculine body trembled and tears rolled down His sober, sensitive face (Luke 19:41). "Oh, Jerusalem," He cried, "what a chance you had and now it is too late" (Luke 19:42).

Before the Lord's inner eye were scenes that would happen nearly forty years later. He saw the destruction of Jerusalem in the year A.D. 70 by the Romans under Titus: "For the days shall come upon thee, that thine enemies shall cast a trench about thee, and compass thee round, and keep thee in on every side" (v. 43), Jesus said.

Four decades later the beseiging Romans built first a timbered earthwork around Jerusalem. But when the Jews destroyed the earthwork, the Romans replaced it with a wall. The historian Josephus tells in detail how Jerusalem was starved out to the point that parents ate their own children. The city finally fell and was leveled to the ground by the enemy. No stone was left on top of another.

No wonder Jesus wept. He loved Jerusalem and He loved His nation. He knew if the people would only accept Him and His message they could escape the horror of a future war and total destruction. Jesus knew what could be and, on the other side, He knew what was to be.

I wonder if Jesus also saw the hill of the skull north of the city toward the east—Golgotha—when He rode over the brow of the mountain? In the present city of Jerusalem is a model of the old Jerusalem with the Herodian temple intact. Every time I stand on the east side of the model I picture myself coming down the Mount of Olives, looking upon the city. If the model is laid out like the old city really was (and I believe it is) the hill of the skull was visible from the top of the Mount of Olives.

Christ knew the end of His triumphant coronation ride. Before His inner eye rose a cross to the sky. He was nailed to it to die—on that hill of Golgotha which nobody paid any attention to—not yet!

We don't know how many heard the Lord's mourning, prophetic words and saw His tears. Only one Gospel writer, Dr. Luke, tells us about it (Luke 19:41-44). People were too happy and excited to listen to sad words. Why spoil a perfect day?

The commotion on the Mount of Olives must have been heard on the Temple mount right across from it. The outer court of the Temple thronged with people. The evening sacrifice was soon to take place and people got into their respective areas to attend it. Jewish men strode toward the court of the men, Jewish women toward the treasury, and Gentiles were gathering in the outer courts, when the word began to spread that Jesus the prophet of Nazareth was on His way to be crowned king (Matthew 21:10,11). The people left the Temple to watch the oncoming procession. No doubt some climbed the Temple walls to see better.

Would the carpenter of Nazareth *really* dare to ride into the Temple? Would He come through the Golden

Gate as the prophets of old foretold? Would the priests crown Him? The excitement grew. People shouted up to the Temple from the nearing procession. Other people picked up the words and passed them along. Everybody began to sing and make happy noises. The only place that was strangely silent was the Temple where, at approximately 3:00 P.M., the priest slayed a lamb and the Temple choir sang to empty walls.

"Everybody is running after that Galilean teacher," the Jewish leaders said in utter disgust (John 12:19). Too bad they didn't listen to the song their choir was singing.

The Jewish people have certain psalms which they sing at various festivals and for each day of the week. The psalm designated for the first day of the week and the evening sacrifice is Psalm 24. (The orthodox Jews still do it today.)

On special festivals two choirs were used. Psalm 24 was divided and one group would sing:

> Lift up your heads, O ye gates;
> And be ye lifted up, ye everlasting doors;
> And the King of glory shall come in.
> Who is the King of glory?

The other choir would answer:

> The Lord of hosts,
> He is the King of glory.

I have no doubt in my mind that Jesus rode through the Golden Gate at just the moment when the choirs were announcing His arrival. The people went wild with joy and anticipation. Children jumped and sang at the top of their lungs (Matthew 21:15).

The Pharisees knew they were losing their power and control over the people. They tried to hush the crowds; they ordered the people back to the Temple service. They told the children to be quiet. But nobody listened. The Pharisees angrily said to Jesus, "Master, do you hear what these children are singing" (Matthew 21:16)? The title master or teacher was used even by His enemies. They had to admit that He was a teacher but they would never have addressed Him as a prophet or as a man who had divine power or authority.

What they actually said was this: "You Galilean teacher, do you *dare* to accept such homage from the children? Who do you think you are? And furthermore, you are endangering all of us by the commotion you are causing. What if the Romans on the walls of the Fortress of Antonia swoop down and punish all of us because they think we are starting a revolution. Now stop this whole nonsense" (John 11:48).

Jesus looked at His enemies and said kindly, "Haven't you read what the Scriptures have to say about this moment (Matthew 21:16)? All heaven and earth have waited for it for a long time. And if these innocent children or My disciples weren't shouting, the stones would cry out" (Luke 19:40).

We don't know what Christ meant when He said the stones might speak up. As science unfolds the mysteries of the earth, we might someday find out that rocks can release sounds, too. Archaeologists revealed that stones speak in many other ways—through carvings and writings preserved for us since ancient times, and by the way we find them arranged.

The stones didn't need to cry out when Christ came into the Temple that day. He came into His own house, but He wasn't received by those who took care of His house (Luke 19:47,48).

Jesus walked into the Temple ahead of the crowd and carefully looked around (Mark 11:11). What He saw filled Him with righteous indignation and sadness. It was the same mess He had seen before. It was again a marketplace, a den of thieves, a place of business and greed, not a prayer house of His heavenly Father.

It was late afternoon. The sacrificial lamb had been slain; the Temple choir had finished. Before the crowd poured in to surround Jesus and announce Him as the new king of Israel, He left quietly and made His way back to Bethany (Mark 11:11). When the shouting multitude arrived, they looked for Him but He was gone.

What a letdown! What a disappointment!

Why had Jesus missed it again? He had spoiled a perfect and golden opportunity to take over and unite the Jews in a revolt against the Romans. Why hadn't He taken advantage of it? Maybe He wasn't so smart after all! Maybe He didn't have what it would take to lead Israel to victory. After all, it was only a carpenter from Nazareth who had ridden a young colt into the Temple. Did it truly have *any* significance? The crowd melted away and night began to settle over Jerusalem.

Little did the people know how long the dark night would last. For many centuries Jerusalem would not see light and Jesus knew it and wept over it (Luke 19:41).

LET'S PRAY: Dear Lord, it is so easy to praise You when things go well and it looks like I am going to get my own way. When You bring my hopes to a different end, I tend to pout and question You. There is nothing new under the sun, is there? I act just as Your disciples did! Please, forgive me when I try to force Your will upon my plans. Teach me to trust You when things don't work out "right," according to my own understanding. As You were able to look beyond when people saw only the present happenings on the day of Your triumphal entry, so can You see now to the end of my earthly life. Please lead me into whatever is best for me in the light of such foresight. I know I would choose Your will if I could see the end from the beginning. I thank You, Jesus, for choosing the cross and not an earthly crown. You did it for me. I love You, Jesus. Amen.

21
WHAT DOES THE FUTURE HOLD?

The day after His triumphal entry Jesus and His disciples set out for Jerusalem again. They obviously stayed in Bethany at night and walked daily to the Temple in Jerusalem. After all, it was only over the hill, less than a mile by a shortcut. It seems that Jesus had not eaten breakfast because the Bible tells us that He was hungry (Mark 11:12). I wonder if He spent the whole night in prayer as He so often did whenever He faced a crisis.

It is most likely that they walked the common road up to the crest of the Mount of Olives and passed Bethphage, "the house of unripe figs." Was it there that Jesus spotted the fig tree afar off and near the road (Mark 11:13)? It wasn't quite yet the time for the harvest of figs. In the favorable climate of Israel the early figs usually ripen by June and the late crop in September.

The time of the Passover probably fell in early April, so it would be a few more weeks before the early fig crops would mature. The tree Jesus noticed was fully leaved. That gave promise of well-developed, though not necessarily ripe fruit, since the fig tree grows leaves and fruit simultaneously. In Oriental lands green or unripe fruit is often eaten as a special treat (Isaiah 28:4).

However, Jesus found nothing except leaves and no traces of fruit. He said to the tree, "You shall never bear any fruit again" (Mark 11:14). The disciples heard Him say it and the Bible does not tell us what anyone thought about it. They went on to Jerusalem and forgot the episode because too many exciting things happened next.

Jesus did something He had done before (vv. 15,16)—He cleansed the Temple again. He drove out the merchants and their customers, He knocked over money tables and sent the money changers running. And He quoted Jeremiah and said, *"My* house shall be called a house of prayer, but you are making it a robber's den" (v. 17; Jeremiah 7:11). Jesus didn't let the business people bring in any more merchandise and He sat down to teach and to heal (v. 17; Matthew 21:14). The blind, crippled and handicapped people, even if they were Jews, were not allowed any farther into the Temple than the outer court. The Jews believed that sickness was a result of sin and a vengeful God doled it out as just punishment to the sinner. Jesus healed them all and perhaps some of these for the first time were allowed to enter the inner Temple courts for prayer. How these people must have praised God and loved Jesus and hung on every word He said.

The chief priests and scribes were furious and felt helpless. They and the businessmen tried to figure out a way to get rid of Jesus, but they were afraid of the people. The crowds listened to Jesus with great enthusiasm and were astonished at His teaching (Mark 11:18).

In the evening the Lord and His disciples left the city as usual to find rest and food in Bethany.

The next morning they walked again to Jerusalem for Jesus taught daily in the Temple (Luke 19:47). As the disciples passed the fig tree which the Lord had cursed, they saw that the tree had dried up from the roots (Mark 11:20). It had died in twenty-four hours and was so noticeable, that Peter said in utter surprise, "Oh, look, Teacher, the tree You cursed yesterday is withered" (v. 21). Why was Peter so surprised? And why did Jesus answer by teaching the principles of absolute faith?

Peter had never seen the Lord perform a miracle in

the negative. To dry up a fruitless tree seemed to be an angry whim. It wasn't like the Master to do such a meaningless thing. But Jesus knew what He was doing. He was a master teacher and knew how to teach in object lessons and parables so that His disciples might never forget what He had taught them.

Jesus looked ahead and knew that His complete rejection by the Jewish leaders was only days away. He knew that by it they brought God's rejection upon themselves. As the withered tree would be cut off and removed, so the Jewish nation would shortly be cut off and destroyed. The Jewish nation was like the fig tree. They had much promise and big words but no fruit to show. They had religious ceremonies and forms of worship but no true godliness.

Jesus had great love and patience for sinners but the most offensive sin to Him was hypocrisy, the vice of the religious leaders of His time (Matthew 23:13-33). He tried to show the disciples that pretentiousness and great display of religious fervor were no substitute for true worship and at no time acceptable before God (Matthew 23:12). Jesus didn't curse other kinds of trees that didn't bear leaves or fruit. These represented the Gentiles who had never claimed or professed to bear fruit for God. They didn't know what the Jews knew and had never been entrusted with the Word of God as Abraham's seed had.

One who receives much from God carries a greater responsibility to share and respond than those who haven't received a special trust (Luke 12:48).

The fig tree pretended! So did the people of Israel.

No doubt the owner of the orchard would have cut the fruitless tree down eventually because it took room away from the other trees. Jesus' miracle speeded up a natural process and showed, at the same time, how fast Israel could wither—and it did. Before all the disciples died the destruction had begun (Matthew 24:2).

The disciples were slow to learn. Instead of perceiving the deep meaning of the visible parable they marveled about the speedy drying up of the tree. Jesus took advantage of their surprise and interest to teach them some important lessons about the prerequisite to answered prayer (Mark 11:22-25). "Your faith can remove mountains," He said (v. 24; Matthew 17:20).

The disciples had a hard time understanding this, just as it was impossible for them to picture a destroyed Temple or city of Jerusalem. "Look, Master," one of His disciples said as they were leaving the Temple, "at the great stones and the beautiful buildings of the Temple" (Matthew 24:1).

The Herodian Temple was the pride and joy of every Jewish heart. Though it wasn't as magnificent and big as Solomon's Temple had been, Josephus (a historian of Christ's time) describes it as an overwhelming structure. He compared the white stone walls to the beauty of a snow-covered mountain and gives us the fabulous size of some of the stones used in the construction. They measured forty-five-by-five-by-six cubits, which is about sixty-six-by-seven-by-nine feet. He also said, "He who has never seen Herod's Temple has never seen beauty."

The construction of the Temple had been going on for almost fifty years (John 2:20) in Christ's time and history tells us that the Jews kept on building on the complex of courts and outer buildings until approximately the year A.D. 63. Seven years after the Temple was finally completed the Roman army of Titus destroyed it totally.

Jesus looked sadly at the magnificent place. "Yes," He said, "look at it while you have a chance. For not one stone will be left upon another, except as ruins" (Matthew 24:2). His answer upset the disciples so deeply that

Peter, Andrew, James and John came to Him privately while He sat on the slopes of the Mount of Olives. Perhaps it happened while they walked back to Bethany at the end of the day and the evening sky had burst into red flames of fire behind the Temple. The snow white walls and gold ornaments of the Temple glowed in the splendor of the dying day. The city looked impregnable, the Temple so mighty that the disciples said, "Lord, when will all those impossible things happen? When will You come back and when will our world end (v. 3)? Will there be some warnings?"

Jesus had explained to the disciples over and over again that He was going to leave them but that He would return. In their minds Christ was still establishing the earthly kingdom of Israel, so they became deeply confused. The Old Testament prophets and other Jewish literature indicated that at the beginning of the Messianic age and His kingdom the present order of things would come to an end. So they could see the end of their world and a new beginning under the reign of the Messiah, but it all appeared so puzzling. They wondered: Would the Herodian Temple have to be destroyed so that the Messiah could build His own? When would it happen? Would it be while Jesus was gone for a while? Would they know the time so they could protect themselves?

Jesus knew that His precious followers with their ingrained Jewish thinking were incapable of grasping the whole concept of His second coming at once. Therefore the Lord blended His answers in such a way that they would later remember and apply His words as the future unfolded. He explained much about the events which would take place before their eyes and in their generation. But He also mixed some prophetic foresights and warnings into it for the benefit of us who live in the shadow of His second coming.

It seemed to the disciples that the fall of Jerusalem and the coming of the Messiah would happen either at the same time or in succession. The Lord didn't divide their thinking. They could not have handled it all at once. He admonished them, "Don't let anyone mislead you (Matthew 24:4). Many will come and claim to be the Messiah (v. 5). There will be wars and revolutions. But that will not be the end, it will only lead toward it. You will see bad famines and epidemics and many earthquakes, and some strange signs in the heavens (vv. 6,7). These happenings must keep you alert because there will come a time when you will be in great danger for your life. You will be persecuted for My name's sake and when the heat is on, many who pretended to love Me will fall away. Their love will grow cold and they will turn on you (vv. 10,12).

"I give you some signs as to the destruction of Jerusalem: when you shall see the city surrounded with armies that set up their idols in the holy place, as Daniel foretold, watch out (Matthew 24:15; Daniel 11:31; 12:11). Leave the city and flee to the mountains and don't hesitate. Hurry out while you have a chance! Time is of the essence (Matthew 24:16-18).

"As to the hour and the date for My coming, nobody knows it, neither men nor angels, nor I, the Son of man. While I live on this earth, I subject Myself to My human limitations and I simply don't know when the Father will send Me back. He alone knows (Matthew 24:36). Though you don't know the date, you can watch the signs. Just as the buds on a fig tree tell you that summer is coming, so the signs I gave you will warn you to watch for My coming" (vv. 32,33).

The Lord spoke of many more things and I am sure that the Holy Spirit brought them to the remembrance of the disciples as they watched the events unfold (John 14:26). They didn't have long to wait. It all happened in their lifetime. Everything came to pass except the second coming of Christ. History tells us that between the time Christ died and the year A.D. 70, when Jerusalem fell, many false prophets appeared and claimed to be the Messiah. Some led groups of Jews into revolts and many wars and insurrections took place. Each revolt was cruelly crushed by the Romans. Famine came in fast succession. A very severe famine is alluded to in Acts 11:28. History puts that famine about A.D. 44 and tells about four famines under the reign of Claudius from A.D. 41-54.

We also know that a series of major earthquakes occurred between A.D. 31-70 in Crete, Rome, Phrygia and Campania, all places in the Roman Empire. Tacitus, a Roman historian, reports about horrible hurricanes and storms in the year A.D. 65.

In A.D. 70 the Roman armies surrounded the city of Jerusalem and set up the symbols of pagan Rome within the Temple area. Josephus is the best historic source for what happened and he tells us that it happened exactly the way Jesus foretold it. Josephus tells about the incredible suffering the Jews experienced while walled in by the enemy. Titus set up the seige while the city was filled with Jews from all over the country. They had come to celebrate the Passover feast. Nobody could leave the city to go back home to their own place. Nobody could enter. Titus shut the city off. There was enough water because Hezekiah's tunnel brought the water inside the city, but food ran out. Again and again Titus asked the Jews to surrender but the Jewish leaders were so convinced they could win in the final moment that they resisted with unreasonable stubbornness. The Christians were caught in the city also, like everyone else.

Unexpectedly the Roman armies retreated temporarily. During that short time the Christians fled. They did what Jesus had told them to do. Supposedly they all fled to the hills east of the Jordan River to a city named Pella. It is said that not one Christian lost his life.

When Titus returned, the city was taken. The Roman soldiers were so infuriated by the stubborn defense of the city that when they finally entered, their wrath and need for revenge knew no limits. The soldiers had orders to spare the Temple but things got out of control. Not only was the Temple sacked but more than one million people perished during and after the seige and ninety-seven thousand Jews were taken captive.

No wonder Jesus wept when He looked at Jerusalem on Palm Sunday. He loved Jerusalem. He still does. He always will. Jerusalem has a special place in God's heart (Zechariah 8:3). Christ's inner eye not only looked to the year A.D. 70 and Jerusalem's destruction, it also looked down the long corridor of time to His second coming and the restoration of Jerusalem as God's holy city.

That which happened on a smaller scale before the fall of Jerusalem will happen all over the earth before the end of the world. How do we know? Because it is happening right *now* before our own eyes.

We see wars and rumors of wars; revolutions and bloodshed are everywhere. The news tells us of many earthquakes, famines and pestilences. Christians are persecuted in more and more countries, while in other places false leaders arise to confuse God's children.

The gospel in Christ's time was preached all over the world within one generation (Acts 17:6). Paul's world was small. When he went to Spain, he had gone to the end of his world.

Now the world is bigger and it takes more effort to spread the gospel. But the good news *is* preached almost everywhere by now.

What should we look for then?

We should look for the final climax of Christ's prophecies when He will appear in the clouds of heaven in glory, surrounded by His angels (Matthew 24:30). He finally will come as the disciples had hoped—as a king (v. 31).

Jesus Christ not only will come as the king of the Jews but as the King of kings and the Lord of lords and as the supreme ruler of heaven and earth (1 Timothy 6:15).

Some Christians find it hard to believe that the second coming of Christ shall be a visible event and true happening. They try to symbolize it away and say we shouldn't take it so literally. But when Christ says something, it *is* real. And when He told His disciples that *every* eye shall see Him, he meant just that (Revelation 1:7). Every eye shall see Him, whether they believe it or not. And every knee shall bow before Him someday and confess that He is Lord (Philippians 2:9-11).

What an exciting time to live in. What a glorious moment to wait for! All we can say is: "Come, Lord Jesus" (Revelation 22:20)!

LET'S PRAY: Yes, Lord Jesus, come and come soon, we are eagerly waiting for You.

I will admit, Jesus, that once in awhile I have wished You would delay Your coming. I get so caught up in my busy life and want to do so many earthly things that I wonder if I will miss something if You come too fast.

Lord, teach me to see with Your eyes. Give me Your mind and heart. If I knew what You know, I couldn't wait to enter Your kingdom. If I truly knew You, Lord Jesus, I would want to see Your face more than anything else on earth. Please give me a new inner vision about Your coming, and please, do come soon. Amen.

22
A FAREWELL DINNER

The day of the Passover celebration had arrived, when the Passover lamb was killed and eaten together with unleavened bread. Since Jesus had no home of His own, He had to depend upon the hospitality of others throughout His whole ministry.

The disciples probably wondered where they would eat the Passover meal, but Jesus knew (Mark 14:13-15). He also knew the deeper meaning of the entire celebration. The Passover was a symbol of Himself (2 Corinthians 5:7).

The Jews didn't know that. They thought the Passover was only in memory of their forefathers' liberation from slavery (Exodus 12:42). In the time of Christ, more than one thousand years after Israel left Egypt, the Passover had become another formal ceremony.

We have no exact historic record on how the Passover was kept during the second temple period, but orthodox Jews still keep the Passover today and Jewish tradition is not given to much change. The Jews are extremely careful not to alter their traditions and symbols from generation to generation. So it seems safe to assume that Jesus and the disciples observed the Passover similar to the way every true Jewish household commemorates it today.

The meal of remembrance is served at the beginning of the day, which begins at sunset for the Jew and ends at sunset the next day. The father or highest in rank is the leader of the ceremony. The table is set in a special way with the Seder plate and goblets for wine.

On the Seder plate we find one roasted shankbone of a lamb, a roasted egg, bitter herbs (horseradish or another harsh vegetable), a piece of parsley, lettuce or celery and a mixture of chopped apples, nuts, dates, cinnamon, ginger and wine. Beside the plate is a pitcher of wine, a bowl of salt water or vinegar and three matzoth (flat unleavened bread).

The shankbone represents the ancient sacrifice of the Passover lamb. We know from Josephus that at Christ's time they roasted a whole lamb and at least ten men had to be present to eat it.

The roasted egg of today takes the place of the sacrifices that were made during Passover day in the Temple. Since the Jews no longer have a Temple, the egg has become a symbol of their mourning for it.

The bitter herbs symbolize the bitter sufferings of Israel under the Egyptian yoke.

The green vegetable is a remembrance of the meager diet of the slaves. It is dipped into the salt water or vinegar, which represents their tears, shed while longing for freedom.

The apple mixture looks like the mortar which was used to build Pharaoh's palaces and pyramids. The unleavened matzoth speaks of their affliction and sudden redemption. Their redemption came upon them so fast, at a time when they least expected it that they did not even have time to let their bread dough rise (Exodus 12:39).

Four glasses of wine are poured and drunk by every participant at various times during the meal. These stand for the four expressions of God's promise to redeem Israel and deliver them from bondage.

Seder means order. The Passover meal is eaten under very strict order and begins when all the participants have reclined for the meal. Today the Jews rest their left elbow on a small pillow. During the time of Christ the

Lord and His disciples reclined in the customary manner of their day (see chapter 20).

The master of the ceremony first pours a glass of wine for everyone. Most likely at the time of Christ a common cup was used from which everyone drank as it was passed around.

The first glass is drunk after the people thank the Lord for bringing them to another Passover. Next, the leader washes his hands, as do all the partakers of the meal. Then he takes pieces of the green vegetables, dips them into the salt water or vinegar and passes them around to everyone. Next he takes the middle loaf of the three matzoth and breaks it. He wraps the larger piece into a cloth and sets it aside. Often it is put under a pillow, almost as though it is buried. The Jews of today believe that they are setting the bread aside for Elijah, the forerunner of the Messiah. They have an extra plate and cup for him every year at the Passover table.

As the father retells the story of deliverance and the family sings traditional songs and reads Scriptures, the second cup is drunk. It is a symbol of God's promise of redemption.

The top loaf and the smaller piece of the broken bread are handed out next and eaten. The green vegetables are dipped a second time and shared together. The third loaf of matzo is used to make two sandwiches, one with the bitter herbs and the other with the apple mixture.

Next the dinner is eaten and after it a closing ceremony takes place. The master takes the large matzo piece that he had set aside. He breaks it and hands a piece to everyone. Much Scripture, prayer and recitation accompanies this part of the ceremony. The people drink the third cup of wine which represents the judgment of God.

The youngest child gets up and opens the door to see if Elijah has arrived. The group sings a song about judgment and then the door is closed.

A final song of thanksgiving closes the Seder. The fourth cup of wine is drunk as a symbol of God's final redemption and as a means of praising Him for it.

When Jesus told the disciples to prepare the Passover meal, He acted in harmony with the custom of His day. He was the Master, the spiritual Father of the group. He was responsible to give the order for preparation of the meal.

The fourteenth day of the month of Nisan is set aside every year to begin the happy feast. Nisan is called, even today, the month of redemption, since in that month Moses led Israel out of Egypt. The Jews also believe that in this month the Messiah will come to them.

The disciples knew all of this and so did Jesus. For the disciples, however, Passover had become a dead form. They observed it on the fourteenth day of Nisan as customary. (The date was the fourteenth day after the new moon, so it did not fall on the same calendar date each year.) They killed and roasted the lamb according to the rules of Moses and sat down and ate in the first hours of the fourteenth day. Tradition tells us that they used the large upper room owned by the mother of John Mark, the Gospel writer. The average peasant home in Jerusalem did not have a room big enough to seat thirteen men. The Bible story suggests that the owner of the upper room must have known Jesus and the disciples and felt friendly toward them (Luke 22:10-12). The disciples were not thinking about the meaning of the ceremony. They settled down after sunset and began to argue about who was the greatest among them (v. 24).

Maybe the argument began when the seating order had to be decided. No doubt everyone wanted to sit on the right side of Jesus for this was the seat of honor. John most likely won for he leaned on the breast of Jesus which suggests that position (John 13:23). We do not know who got to sit on the left side. We know that Peter sat next to John. Did Judas elbow himself to the left side, I wonder? He sat close to the Lord, close enough to receive the first morsel Christ handed out (v. 26).

After everyone finally sat down on his cushion, grumbling and full of jealousy, the Lord poured the first cup of wine and broke the middle loaf of matzo, and set it aside. Nobody knew what He was doing; they were too full of resentment. Tenderly Jesus tried to bring them around. "I have looked forward to this meal with deep longing," He said quietly. "This is the last meal we eat together until we dine again in My Father's kingdom" (Luke 22:16).

The disciples didn't hear. They were too busy glaring at John and each other.

Jesus stood up. Instead of washing His own hands and letting them wash their hands in the usual ceremonial way, He got up from His cushion, laid aside His garments and dressed Himself like a servant with a towel. Then, He began to wash His disciples' feet.

Usually a guest's feet were washed by a slave as the guest entered someone's house for a feast or banquet. Since there was no servant available that night, one of the disciples should have been willing to at least wash the Master's feet! But nobody did. It would have marked him as lowest in position. Still believing that Christ would soon erect His earthly kingdom, they already saw themselves as high officials in the new government. Acting as a slave would have suggested that they were not fit to become top dignitaries.

I wonder whose feet Christ washed first? Maybe He started with Judas. Lovingly He washed the dust from the feet of a man who would lift his heel against Him that same night (John 13:27). Then He dried them carefully with a towel. Did the Lord's loving eyes plead with Judas to repent while He did it? Was Christ still trying to save His erring follower from eternal condemnation?

The disciples watched as Jesus went from cushion to cushion to perform His humiliating, menial task. They were speechless, stunned, ashamed and overwhelmed.

Peter, as usual, broke the silence. "Lord," he said, "You'd better not wash my feet! This isn't Your job. You are the Lord. You are above all of us" (John 13:6-8).

Jesus might have smiled. Good, old, impulsive Peter, when would he ever learn the *true* meaning of an outward action? "Peter," the Lord said, "you'd better let me wash your feet or you can't be my partner anymore" (v. 8).

"If you insist, then You'd better wash all of me—my hands, my head . . . " (v. 9)! Peter did his usual thing; He tried to tell his Lord what to do and how to do it better.

Jesus perhaps smiled His loving patient smile again. "Peter," He said, "the feet are enough" (v. 10).

Peter couldn't see it then but later he understood. He saw the deeper meaning and the new, special truth in Christ's words and actions (1 Peter 5:1-3).

The Lord was not so concerned about a bit of dust on the sandaled feet of His disciples as He was about the dirt in their souls. Their jealousy and resentment needed to be washed away—and nobody can cleanse himself. Christ is the only one who can wash away sins.

By the time the Lord had made His round, His purpose for that final meeting had been accomplished. The disciples were ashamed, repentant, and ready to listen and to be taught—all except one.

"You are clean," the Lord said when He sat down again to continue the Passover celebration, "but that isn't true of everyone here" (John 13:10). I wonder what Judas thought when Christ knelt before him to wash his feet? Was he tempted to confess? Was an evil demon already so deeply in control that Judas only got angry? After all, what undignified behavior for a future king!

Would this Galilean peasant ever learn to do things properly?

"Do you *understand* what I just did?" Christ said after He robed and seated Himself. "You call Me, Lord and Master, and I am that. Now, if *I* served you as I just did, you had better learn to do the same thing. I have shown you an example to follow. The greater you want to be, the more you need to be willing to minister to each other" (vv. 13-17).

The Lord handed out the bitter herbs and the pieces of matzo and they began to eat the meal together. "One of you will betray Me," the Lord said while they ate.

Peter motioned to John to find out who Jesus was talking about (v. 24). It couldn't be one of the disciples, or could it?

Jesus said, "The one to whom I hand the food, he is the one."

He handed a piece of bread or vegetable to Judas, and then also to the rest of the group. The disciples were horrified. "It isn't I, Lord, is it?" each one asked (Matthew 26:22).

Judas never said a word. All eyes at last must have focused on him, the only one who had never asked the question. Judas acted innocently, "It isn't I, Master, is it?" he said nonchalantly. He didn't call Him, Lord.

Jesus answered, "Thou hast said" (Matthew 26:25). He said neither yes or no. What divine tact. What love and compassion! The Lord tried to save face for Judas while letting him know that he could not keep his scheming secret from Him.

So tactful was the Master that when He finally said, "You better hurry and do it now," and Judas got up and left, the other disciples thought that Judas had been sent on an errand for the group (John 13:27-29).

I have no doubt that it was after the meal at the closing ceremony that Christ initiated the new ordinances of the Lord's Supper. He took the piece of matzo which had been laid aside wrapped up in a cloth, broke it and said, "This is My body, which is given for you. Eat it" (Luke 22:19). Then He poured the third cup of wine which represented the judgments of God. "This is My blood," He said, as He gave it to the disciples and they sipped the deep red wine, "poured out to forgive the sins of many" (Matthew 26:27,28).

What symbolism. What deep meaning the Jews carry in their Passover meal! The three matzoth loaves picture the Godhead: Father, Son and Holy Spirit, the middle loaf broken, wrapped in a cloth—the Son of God, wrapped in burial linen, laid aside for the resurrection with His blood covering a sinful world against judgment and condemnation.

"Whenever you break this ceremonial bread and drink the wine, look back and remember My death," the Lord said while He poured the fourth cup. "But it is not all sad; I am coming back. So also look forward and rejoice because I am returning to you someday" (Matthew 26:29; 1 Corinthians 11:26).

So the disciples, shaken, confused and worried, stood up and joined their voices with the Lord's in a song of praise while they drank the last cup of wine together. After that they could, customarily, eat and drink no more during the rest of the night until morning.

The cup of praise was the climax of an evening they would never ever forget as long as they lived.

Nobody but Jesus knew what was ahead as they left the upper room that night. Nobody but Him—and He sang a hymn of praise to His Father after He broke the bread and poured the wine!

LET'S PRAY: Dear Jesus, Your love and tact and example overwhelm me. How can I ever understand the depth of Your teachings? I am so much like Your impulsive Peter was. I speak up at the wrong time. I tell You what to do and how to do it. But like Peter I mean well. You know my heart, Jesus. You know it better than I do and I am glad.

It doesn't come easily to my nature to wash somebody else's feet. My feelings get hurt so often and I feel put down. Teach me true greatness, my Lord, and help me to find deep joy in serving others. Lord, may I glorify Your name by praising You when things look dark. Let me follow Your example all the way, and let me be kind even to those who betrayed my trust. You did it with Judas. How can I help but love You, my wonderful Lord. Amen.

23
FRIEND—
HOW CAN
YOU DO THIS?

Jesus knew that time was soon running out and He tried to prepare His followers for His departure. In Jewish culture a father gave his son the birthright and a special blessing just before he died. So Jesus gave His "children" a final blessing and special instructions. But they didn't know it. Would they have listened better if they had known that these were His parting words before His death?

Only John remembered well enough later to write His words down for us. No other Gospel writer records the details or the prayer Jesus prayed while they walked toward the Mount of Olives. I am so glad that John listened for I believe that the Lord's recorded words in the fourteenth, fifteenth, sixteenth and seventeenth chapters of John are some of the most important messages Jesus ever gave. Every sentence has so much meaning that we will study all of these teachings in the next course. (See *Learn of Me*, another Bible study.)[1]

Most of the disciples perhaps were too confused and upset to listen closely, at least that night. Jesus had said so many disturbing things. First, He had suggested that one of them would betray Him. Next, He had announced that He was going to leave them soon (John

13:33). Then He seemed to contradict Himself. How could Jesus go away and yet say, "Without Me, you can do nothing" (John 15:5)? And what did He mean with His promise that He would send the Comforter, the Holy Spirit, and they should be glad that He was going away (John 16:7)?

They didn't want someone else in Christ's place. They wanted to be with Him and become top leaders in the new revolutionary Jewish government—right next to Him.

Would He call for the revolt against the Romans by morning light? Where was the Master going? When would He do the expected thing? Peter asked the question pointedly as they left the upper room, "Master, where are You going" (John 13:36)?

Jesus gave a mysterious answer: "You can't go with Me now," He said quietly, "but you will follow Me later" (v. 36).

Peter did his usual thing. He tried to straighten out the Lord's thinking. "Why can't I go with You now?" Peter said with a big flair, "I would go even if I had to die for you!"

Jesus shook His head and said sadly, "Simon, Simon, you don't know yourself at all" (Luke 22:31). Jesus called him Simon twice, not by his new name, Peter. To double a name or word meant to give it great emphasis. It would be the old nature of the impulsive, fickle, fearful Simon bar-Jona who would do what Peter, the disciple of Christ, the rock, had no intention of doing.

"You *all* will desert Me tonight," Jesus said to His eleven followers, "as was prophesied in the Scriptures" (Mark 14:27; Zechariah 13:7).

Peter's chest stuck out in confidence. "I will never desert You," he said confidently and waved toward the other disciples. "No matter what they will do, I will stick by You" (Mark 14:29).

Jesus said kindly, "Peter, I want to tell you something: between now and tomorrow morning when the rooster crows twice, you will have denied Me three times and declared that you don't even know Me" (v. 30).

Peter was beside himself, "No," he exploded, "I'll never do such a thing, even if I have to die with You!" And all the other men assured Jesus of the same loyalty (v. 31), while Peter and another disciple clutched a sword (Luke 22:38).

The city of Jerusalem was filled with people and nobody noticed anything unusual about twelve men conversing and walking out of the city in order to find shelter and a place to rest for the night. The Lord directed His steps across the Kidron Valley and entered a grove of olive trees called the Garden of Gethsemane. He told the disciples, "You stay here while I go and pray" (Mark 14:32). Many times before, Jesus and the disciples had gone there, so it wasn't anything unusual (John 18:1,2).

However, this time He took Peter, James and John with Him into a more secluded place and said, "Wait here and watch with Me. My soul is crushed by sorrow to the point of death. Don't leave Me alone in this" (Mark 14:34). He walked just a stone's throw away from them (v. 35), but He must have been within sight and hearing of some of the disciples, for we know what happened next.

Jesus fell face downward to the ground, showing signs of a strange sadness, horror and deep distress. "My Father!" He cried out, "if it is possible let this cup pass from Me. Nevertheless I want to do Your will, not Mine." Jesus' prostrated form convulsed in such agony of spirit that He broke out into a sweat like drops of blood (Luke 22:44).

Three times He repeated the same prayer. Three

times He walked, perhaps staggered, toward His three prayer partners—and found them asleep or nearly asleep. "Can't you even stand by Me for one hour with your prayers?" He asked. "And if you can't pray for Me, pray for yourselves. You are heading for big temptations and though your spirit thinks you are strong, your body is weak" (Matthew 26:41).

But the disciples slept and Jesus was left to struggle alone when He needed human sympathy and tender friendship the most.

What made Jesus agonize so in sorrow? Was Jesus suddenly afraid to die a human death? Hardly! He knew that He had come to this earth to live and die as a human being. He also knew that He didn't have to submit Himself to His enemies unless He wanted to. He could deliver Himself if He saw fit (v. 53).

What cup shook mysteriously in His trembling hand when He begged His Father to let it pass by? The word "cup" is a common Bible figure for suffering or punishment (Isaiah 51:17; Jeremiah 49:12; Lamentations 4:21; Psalms 11:6; 16:5). What punishment seemed unbearable to Jesus?

Jesus knew He was just about to become the bearer of the sins of the world. His sinless nature recoiled from sin, for He knew no sin. He had never sinned, and He had never been in disharmony with His heavenly Father. "The Father and I are one" (John 10:30), He could say. And He had assured His disciples on the way to Gethsemane with the words, "You shall leave Me alone, and yet, I am not alone, because the Father is with Me" (John 16:32).

Jesus knew who He was and what was His to claim. He was the sinless, divine/human Son of God and He carried eternal life within Himself. The only thing Jesus didn't know was what would happen when He suddenly became a sinner in God's eyes. Sin had never stood between Him and His Father. He didn't know the consequences of such a happening.

I have no doubt that Satan troubled and tortured the Lord for days with suggestions that sin meant eternal separation from God. Now in the discouraging human loneliness of a pitch black, chilled midnight hour Satan pressed his ugly cruel suggestion into the Saviour's soul and nearly crushed Him.

What if God's nature couldn't tolerate sin, even on a sinless sin-bearer? What if the price Jesus paid cost Him eternal separation from the One He loved so deeply? "Father, if *that* is Your will, I'll do it. Your will be done." As Jesus prayed, the thought caused Him to sweat great drops.

"Wasn't anyone there to comfort Him? Though no human being understood His agony and grief, His Father did, He finally sent an angel to comfort and strengthen His Son (Luke 22:43). I am sure the heavenly visitor wiped the Lord's brow and gave Him a special message from the Father above so that Jesus felt new strength and calmness.

He needed it, for He heard noises in the distance. He got up from the cold ground where the olive trees had dripped wet dew on Him, as if all nature wept over their Creator's agony, and walked over to the disciples.

"Are you still sleeping and resting?" Jesus said. "The time has come to get up and get ready. The man who is going to betray Me is coming" (Matthew 26:45).

Yes, Judas knew where to find the Master. A group of Temple police and a multitude of armed men followed the traitor, lighting the dark night with blazing torches and lanterns. No doubt, some curious rabble rousers also had followed, eager to see what was going on and looking for cheap excitement.

Jesus did not run or flinch. He stepped out toward them and said, "Who are you looking for" (John 18:4)?

"Jesus of Nazareth," they answered.

"I am He," He said calmly. As He said it, they all fell backward to the ground (v. 6). The Bible does not tell us why everyone toppled over, but I am sure that a supernatural power shone out of Jesus when He said, "*I am.*" His divinity flashed for a moment and people fell flat. He could have used that moment of confusion to escape, but He didn't. He chose to stay.

The people scrambled back to their feet and Jesus asked once more, "Who are you looking for?"

They repeated, "Jesus of Nazareth."

"I told you that I am He," Jesus said, "and since I am the one you are looking for, let these others go" (v. 8). His words again fulfilled Bible prophecy (v. 9; John 17:12).

The soldiers didn't move. They did not believe that the one who spoke was truly Jesus of Nazareth. Who would voluntarily admit under cover of night that He was the one they were looking for? They also had to wait, according to Jewish law, for someone to accuse Him before they could arrest Him.

Judas had told the men, "You will know which one to arrest when I go over and kiss Him. Then you can take Him easily." So now Judas walked up to Jesus and embraced Him with a great show of affection. He kissed Him on the cheek and said, "Hail, Master" (Matthew 26:49)!

This kind of greeting was a common mode of exchanging affection among friends. Even today we find Eastern men greet each other that way.

Jesus looked into the traitor's face. "Friend," He said kindly, "how can you do this, betray the Master with a *kiss*" (v. 50)? He called him, "friend." Jesus didn't scold. He didn't remind Judas of all the kind things he had received from His hand. They had eaten together. He did not even say, "Judas, just a few hours ago I washed your feet just because I loved you so." With that one word Jesus spoke a whole sermon. He said, "Judas, it hurts that it had to be *you* who betrayed Me. My betrayal had to come but why did *you* have to lend yourself to it? It hurts so much more because you used a *kiss* to do it. If you had just pointed or thrown a rock at Me, it would have been easier. Why must you add hypocrisy to your betrayal. I prefer honest hate to pretended love. Your kiss hurts more than that you agreed to deliver Me into the hands of My enemies!"

Without resistance Jesus let Himself be bound while His disciples and perhaps even Judas watched in speechless horror. They all *knew* He could free Himself; why didn't He?

Peter acted according to his normal philosophy of life: When in doubt, *do or say something*, even if it is something foolish! So he drew his sword and struck out. He didn't aim very good but he managed to do some damage. He slashed off the right ear of Malchus, the High Priest's servant (John 18:10).

Jesus said to Peter, "Put your sword away. This is not My way of fighting. If I wanted to fight, I could call all heaven for help. Look, I am doing what My Father wants Me to do" (Matthew 26:53,54). Then Jesus touched the man's bleeding cut and restored the ear. Did He reach up with bound hands to do His last healing miracle? Had Malchus helped to bind Him? The Bible doesn't tell the details but once more Jesus gave people a chance to see and believe. They didn't!

Then Jesus spoke to the crowd: "Why did you come after Me with swords and clubs? Am I a dangerous criminal? I was among you daily in the Temple teaching and healing and you didn't touch Me. You know that I haven't done anything you could arrest Me for in public, so you are doing it secretly in the night. But this is all happening to fulfill the words of the prophets as recorded in the Scriptures" (Matthew 26:56; Psalm 41:9).

The disciples had watched and listened up to this point, waiting for Jesus to deliver Himself and them. It now dawned on them, perhaps clearly for the first time, that the Master had no intention of doing as they expected. Was He truly going to do as He had said and let Himself be killed? If so, the followers of a condemned leader were often killed by the Romans, too.

Peter forgot his brave promise he had given just a few hours before and so did the other disciples. They stepped back under the dark trees and turned to run into the night. Yes, *all* the disciples forsook Him and fled (Matthew 26:56).

Jesus was led away, bound and surrounded by cruel men—and one lone figure watched the group walk away. He listened to their cheers of glee and delight because they had found and arrested Jesus. And in the ears of Judas rang the words: "Friend—how can you do this?"

LET'S PRAY: Dear Jesus, You are still so often betrayed with a kiss and pretended love by Your followers. So many profess allegiance and call you Lord, but sell You out whenever they cannot force You to do things their way.

Please, let me never do this to You, even if my own heart would want to deceive me by clever rationalization.

Lord, an honest atheist has a better chance to find You than a religious pretender. You cannot help hypocrites, can You? It isn't that You don't want to, but they will not let You.

Judas didn't let Your kindness melt his stony heart, even when You called him, friend.

Oh, help me never to be a pretender or hard-hearted. May I forever be Your true friend and never forsake

You—ever! I love You, Jesus, even though I often do foolish things like Peter. But I do love You in spite of myself, because You loved me first. Amen.

Footnote

1. Maria Anne Hirschmann, *Learn of Me* (Huntington Beach, CA: Hansi Ministries, Inc., 1979).

24
CRUCIFY HIM!

The Jewish law of Christ's time made it clear that a person was innocent until proven guilty. To be brought to trial one had to have an accuser. In the trial at least two or three witnesses had to agree completely for or against the accused prisoner before the judge and the jury could proceed.

When Jesus was arrested, probably around midnight, His enemies had no intention of giving Him a fair trial or giving Him an opportunity to prove His innocence. They had come to a verdict a long time ago! Jesus of Nazareth had to *die* (John 7:1).

Their problem was that they couldn't do the murdering themselves. They had lost the right to inflict capital punishment on anyone: the Romans were the only ones who could sentence to death. The Roman government prided itself, according to the historian Josephus, in that it gave lawful trials and was just and fair even with their foreign subjects. So, it was obvious that the Jewish leaders had a problem on their hands, but they were determined to accomplish their goal. Jesus' arrest came at a very inconvenient time: the city was full of people and many of Jesus' followers from the north had come to celebrate the Passover and the Feast of Unleavened Bread. Jesus had many friends among the common people, and even in the Sanhedrin, some leaders had spoken up twice in His defense (John 7:45,50,51; 12:42). For the sake of those who were favorable toward Him, a certain form of legality had to be kept. The Romans also had to be convinced that the Jews' verdict was just. So the soldiers had orders to bring their prisoner to Annas, the father-in-law of Caiaphas, who was high priest that year (John 18:13). He was the one who had declared, "Better that *one* should die for all" (v. 14).

Annas had been high priest of the Jews before Caiaphas and was in age and rank the one honored and respected for his position. But every year the Romans sold the office of high priest to the highest bidder and obviously Caiaphas had outbid his father-in-law. But would Caiaphas be experienced enough to handle such a touchy trial? Annas had the experience and perhaps knew the loopholes of the law better—so why not begin with him?

Annas lost no time and began questioning Jesus as soon as He was brought in. He hoped to trick Jesus into some answers which could be used against Him, suggesting that Jesus was starting something in secret and gathering a silent following against the government. Jesus silenced Annas with overwhelming logic and tactfully pointed out that he was breaking the Jewish law. "Why are you asking *Me* that question?" Jesus said (v. 21). With it He reminded Annas that in Jewish law nobody could be sentenced by his own personal witness or words alone, but by two or three outside witnesses who had to agree (Hebrews 10:28; Deuteronomy 17:6; 19:15).

"Ask those who heard Me," Jesus suggested (John 18:21). This was something Annas wouldn't want to do at any cost for those who heard Jesus believed Him (John 10:40-42).

Annas failed to prove anything and hastened to send the prisoner to his son-in-law, Caiaphas.

Caiaphas was waiting and with him waited the entire Jewish supreme court. They even brought in many witnesses to testify against Jesus (Matthew 26:59,60). The Sanhedrin had assembled for a night trial. Not every member of the governing body had to be present, only a majority was needed. I have no doubt in my mind that the sly leaders had only those present who wouldn't oppose their unscrupulous plans. They had broken their own laws already by sitting in judgment over a capital case at night. Capital charges could only be tried and concluded by day.

The witnesses contradicted each other and the trial was getting nowhere. Caiaphas got more and more nervous and tense. He knew that something had to be done before the city awakened and the message got around that Jesus had been condemned. Two witnesses had a resemblance of agreement, but even their words were not enough to build a case (v. 61). Jesus didn't defend Himself at all (v. 63). Caiaphas finally stood up.

"I demand in the name of the living God an answer from You. Are You the Messiah, the Son of God" (v. 63)?

Jesus had to answer this request or deny the existence of God. "Yes," Jesus said, "I am" (v. 64).

What a statement then was made by one who supposedly was being judged. "I am going to come some day to judge the world, including you, as the Son of God," He said matter-of-factly and without fear. This statement couldn't be ignored by the Jewish leaders even if some were willing to let Him go. Christ forced them by His statement to make a decision.

Caiaphas got so aggravated by Jesus' answer that he tore his own clothing. This was supposed to be a sign of condemnation and passing judgment after proven guilt (v. 65). The Mosaic law prohibited the high priest from tearing his garments (Leviticus 10:6; 21:10). "Blasphemy," he shouted. "What need do we have for other witnesses?"

Unfortunately he *did* have need of other witnesses, but since he couldn't find any, he used Christ's own words against Him and broke another Jewish law in the process.

The court unanimously sentenced Jesus to death (Matthew 27:1). Now they had to wait until daytime to proceed. The Sanhedrin had to reaffirm their decision by daylight and they had to see the Roman governor, whom they didn't dare wake before morning. The Bible does not tell us where Jesus spent the hours between the moment the verdict was reached and the time they took Him to Pilate. At that time Pilate was the procurator appointed by Caesar over Judea.

Archaeological findings in the Jewish quarters of the old city of Jerusalem have identified the house of Caiaphas. It is a typical home of a wealthy Jew of Christ's time and beneath the surface are two prisons, again very typical for that time period. One prison, called the open prison, was used to hold those who awaited trial or had to stay there for minor offenses. The other prison, called the deep prison or the pit, held prisoners who were condemned to death. The entrance to it was through a hole in its top where the prisoner was let down by a rope.

One cannot help but wonder, did they keep Jesus in that deep pit until daybreak? We know that He was led out of Caiaphas' courtyard shortly after daybreak because something happened just as the roosters began to crow: Jesus turned and looked at Peter (Luke 22:61).

John and Peter, after their initial flight, decided to find out what was happening to their Master. John knew the high priest and was permitted to be at the place of the trial (John 18:15).

Peter didn't have the same influence and stood outside Caiaphas' gate. So John saw to it that Peter got permission to enter the courtyard. Three times Peter was asked if he was a follower of Jesus and three times

Peter denied it. The third time he took drastic measures and cursed and swore to prove he wasn't. Followers of Jesus didn't swear or use the name of God in vain, so Peter did it to prove his point.

A rooster crowed a second time as Jesus was brought into the courtyard. The embers of a night fire smoldered into gray ashes and the new morning light permitted people to look into each other's faces and see their expression. Jesus looked at Peter—and Peter left the courtyard and found a quiet place to cry his heart out. He remembered what Jesus had said to him (Mark 14:72).

While Peter wept, a distressed figure stormed into the Sanhedrin's trial shouting, "Stop everything! I'll give you the money back. I have sinned for I betrayed an innocent man" (Luke 22:62). Judas perhaps realized that his scheme had backfired. He didn't mean to betray Jesus into death but to force Him into action. But Jesus was not taking action, He was letting Himself be led like a lamb to the slaughter, without protest or opening His mouth to defend His innocence (Isaiah 53:7). "Please don't do it! I have done a great wrong in being His accuser," Judas pleaded.

"That's your problem," the leaders retorted.

Judas threw the thirty pieces of silver before them and stormed out—to hang himself.

Two men betrayed Jesus. One wept, the other committed suicide. Was Judas' sin greater than Peter's? No, both of them let Jesus down. But one repented genuinely and the other was sorry for the wrong outcome, not the sin itself. Judas took judgment into his own hands and his death became known all over the city. He died in an ugly manner (Acts 1:18).

The money Judas returned bought a field and fulfilled prophecy again (v. 19; Psalms 69:25; 109:8).

Meanwhile Christ was brought by the Jewish leaders

before Pilate. Pilate and the Jews were not on the best of terms according to Josephus; and the Gospels also read that way between the lines. The Jews brought Jesus to the Roman governor to ask for His death.

Pilate usually stayed in Caesarea but during major Jewish festivals all the Roman officials took up residence in Jerusalem since the danger of revolt and insurrection was at its highest during these times.

"What is your charge against this man?" Pilate asked (John 18:29).

The Jewish leaders had no charge. "We wouldn't have brought Him to you if He weren't a criminal in our eyes," they answered hoping to bluff Pilate.

"Well, then, do the whole thing yourselves," Pilate answered clearly showing irritation by his answer.

"But we want Him crucified," they said, "and we need your approval." Jews didn't crucify; they stoned. They were not above Pilate's suggestion to take justice into their own hands, as we see later at the death of Stephen whom they stoned without Roman help (Acts 7:57). But they didn't dare to do it that morning. The Romans were on alert and the crowds might not be willing to stone Jesus.

Pilate went inside to question Jesus. The Jews stayed outside his house so they wouldn't defile themselves. If they had entered the house of a Gentile they would not be permitted to eat the final meal of the Passover day, which entered them into the Feast of Unleavened Bread (v. 28).

What irony! To step into Pilate's house would be a defilement; to plot the murder of an innocent man left them "purified" in their own eyes.

"Are You the King of the Jews?" Pilate asked Jesus (v. 33).

" 'King,' as *you* use the word or as the Jews use it?" Jesus asked back (v. 34, ***TLB***).

Pilate felt aggravated. The prisoner showed no sign of fear and acted as if He had control over the whole thing. "Am I a Jew?" Pilate exploded. "Your people brought You to me. What have You done?"

Jesus said with quiet dignity, "I am not an earthly king. If I were, I wouldn't stand before you but be out there leading a revolution. My kingdom is different" (v. 36).

Pilate looked at Jesus' royal bearing and His peaceful, fearless behavior. "But You *are* a king?" he asked.

"Thou sayest," Jesus said. Throughout the entire trial the only questions Jesus answered were those involving His Messiahship. He claimed to be the Son of God and the King of the Jews. With these claims He practically *forced* both governments to act. The first was considered blasphemy by the Jews. The second an act of treason by the Romans.

Jesus tried to awaken in Pilate a hunger for the spiritual things He had to offer. "I came to bring truth," Jesus explained.

"What is truth?" Pilate exclaimed and went outside.

Pilate had no time to philosophize with a Jewish prisoner, but he knew that Jesus was a harmless, innocent man. He said so several times (John 18:38; 19:4,12; Luke 23:14,22). The whole deal was most unpleasant to him. If he gave in and did what the Jews asked him to do, he not only could get in trouble with Caesar for unjust cruelty but also with his wife. She had sent an urgent message to him (Matthew 27:19). On the other hand the Jews threatened to report him to Caesar if he didn't condemn the man. What a tight spot to be in. Well, maybe he didn't have to make a decision. Jesus came from Galilee. Why not send Him to Herod Antipas, the Roman governor of Galilee who also had come to Jerusalem to be on hand in case of an emergency (Luke 23:7).

Herod was delighted to see Jesus. He had heard so much about Him. It pleased the Roman so much that he buried his grudge against Pilate that day and they became friends. Or, at least accomplices in crime. So often bad causes can bring opposite sides together. It worked for the Sadducees and the Pharisees who never saw eye to eye on anything until they united to condemn Jesus. What a reason to become friends.

Herod questioned his prisoner and hoped to see a miracle, but Jesus never said a word. Outside the Jewish leaders stood and shouted their accusations (vv. 8-10). Herod felt put down and his authority questioned. He and his soldiers started to mock the Lord and put a kingly robe on Him. Maybe it was an old robe of Herod's, a faded purple and a bit torn. They made fun of Jesus and finally sent Him back to Pilate because they couldn't get any reaction out of the Man, either by cruelty or mockery. Herod was rather afraid of Jesus anyway. He wondered if He was John, whom he had killed, risen again.

Pilate was afraid of Jesus, too. The message from his wife disturbed him greatly and he wanted to get out of the situation but he couldn't. He had to do what any person has to do: make a clear decision for or against Jesus. Pilate thought he could stay in the middle.

"Look," he said, "I give you Jews a choice. Every holiday I release one of your prisoners. Do you want Barabbas or Jesus, your King?"

"Release Barabbas and crucify Jesus," the mob shouted, excited and stirred up by the Jewish leaders (v. 18).

Pilate tried to reason with them for awhile and then he called for a bowl of water. "I wash my hands in innocence," he said, using a Jewish custom to make his point. "The responsibility is yours" (Matthew 27:24).

"Crucify Him," the mob raged. "Kill Him. Crucify Him!"

So Pilate released Barabbas the murderer and rebel and handed Jesus over to be crucified (v. 26)!

LET'S PRAY: Dear Jesus, I have heard and read the story of Your trial and death many times. I am afraid that it is such a familiar story that I never saw the depth of it.

Lord, I get upset when I am treated the least bit unfairly by others. I know I have a long way to go before I can take abuse as You did. And You were treated harshly for my sake that I may be treated kindly for Your sake. Oh Jesus, it overwhelms me when I think how badly You were treated for being good. Remind me when I get defensive and uptight that You blessed those who suffer for righteousness sake. Make me willing to be made willing to take abuse and criticism when I don't deserve it. You took so much for me and You still do. The world still treats You as unfairly as they did in Pilate's court. And You are still as patient and eager to teach truth as You were when Pilate asked You. Teach me, my Lord, for Your name's sake. Amen.

25
IT IS FINISHED!

"Behold the Man," Pilate said, hoping He would evoke the pity of the Jewish people (John 19:5).

There Jesus stood before the mob with a robe over His bleeding back, His flesh raw from the heavy beatings. Scourging was done with whips that had pieces of metal tied to the ends of each strand. It was so cruel a punishment that no Roman citizen could be beaten that way. No Roman citizen could be crucified either. Only non-Romans were treated in such torturous, inhuman fashion. One flogging often killed a man and Jesus might have been beaten twice. Roman soldiers had made a crown from thorny twigs and pressed it on their prisoner's head.

"Behold the Man," Pilate said and didn't know what a magnificent statement he made.

The King of the universe had become Man, all human, and He stood before mankind to die a human death. On His thorn-pierced, blood-stained head He wore a type of wreath similar to the one the Roman emperor wore when he entered Rome after great victories.

The mob beheld "the Man" and went into a raging frenzy. He stood there, pale and exhausted from lack of sleep, loss of blood and miles of walking. Lines of suffering etched His noble face, but He had the bearing of a King. He made not *one* gesture to them which pleaded for mercy. He showed no trace of fear or intimidation. He seemed to be in complete peace; more than that, He seemed to be in utter control of the whole situation: He had been in control all through the trial and condemnation, to the point where He had assured Pilate that he had no power over Him (Jesus) but that which was given to him from above (v. 11).

There is nothing more irritating to weak people who are in authority than when someone questions their power and strength. Jesus did just that in His silent detachment and obvious unconcern to save Himself. No doubt, Satan and all his evil powers were among the multitudes also, whipping up their hellish hate.

"Crucify Him," and "We have no other king but Caesar," they screamed (v. 15). Their eagerness to get rid of Jesus was so great that they betrayed their most treasured doctrine—their belief that a Messiah would come to lead them back to independence and glory.

Roman soldiers now took their prisoner and prepared Him for crucifixion. They had a game called "the game of the king." For it they had some lines etched into the pavement. (These etchings can be seen today in the old city of Jerusalem. They are below the Sisters of Zion convent, where the original stones of Pilate's judgment hall were discovered by accidental digging.) In that game soldiers would dress up a prisoner as a king, blindfold him and then beat, abuse and mock him and demand that he guess who was hurting him. A long straight line pointed the direction in which a prisoner was led away—*always* to crucifixion.

The place of crucifixion, according to the Gospel writers, was outside the city walls, on a hill called *Golgotha*, which means "skull" (v. 17).

Today there are two places that are designated as that holy place. The Catholic church believes that Golgotha or Calvary (after the Greek word, *kranion*, which means skull) was the crucifixion hill. This is where the Church of the Holy Sepulchre stands today. Some of the Protestant world believes the hill was Gordon's Calvary. According to the Old Testament Scripture Gordon's

Calvary is more likely the place for we find it outside the walls of the second Temple period and north of the Temple altar where the burnt offerings were slain (Leviticus 1:11). Nobody knows for sure where the crucifixion took place, but we know something about the method by which it was carried out.

Contrary to most pictures which have been painted since Christ's death, the prisoner did not carry the whole cross but only the cross bar. The upright piece was at the place of execution and was used over and over again. The prisoner's outstretched arms were tied to the crossbar and he carried the wood in that awkward position to the place he was to die (John 19:17).

The burden of the heavy piece of wood across the lacerated, bruised and swollen back proved too much for the human strength of the Man Jesus. Since He never used His divinity to help Him out in times of need but lived only by the resources any human being may have, He finally fell. Tradition tells us that He fell twice. How does a human form fall when his outstretched arms are tied to a heavy piece of wood? Since He had no hands to break His fall, He either fell straight on His face or backward on top of the crude splintering wood while the thorns pressed deeper into His brow.

The soldiers must have done their best to whip Him up again, but Jesus' body had no more muscle strength left. He had not eaten since the last supper at sundown the night before. He most likely had not slept at all. After His last free walk from the Upper Room to the Garden of Gethsemane, the soldiers had walked Him to the house of Annas then to Caiaphas. Next He was taken to the Fortress of Antonia to appear before Pilate in the judgment hall. Then, they led Him to the citadel where Herod stayed for the Passover. Herod sent Him back to Pilate. There they finally prepared Him for execution.

We do not know the exact time when Christ was taken to the place of death. Mark tells us that the process of crucifixion began at 9:00 in the morning (Mark 15:25). Most likely it was soon after this that He arrived at Calvary. The Jews were eager to hurry things up for they knew it was the day before Sabbath. Even if the Passover fell on a day other than Friday, the day after was always a ceremonial Sabbath (Leviticus 23:5-7).

It was against Jewish law to carry out the death sentence the same day it was pronounced. Therefore the Jewish court never declared capital punishment on a day prior to a Sabbath, be it the weekly or ceremonial Sabbath day. These leaders found themselves in a great predicament and suddenly had to do things they had tried to avoid (Matthew 26:3-5). Not only did they have to break many of their judicial traditions and laws, but they had to be aware of the crowds. Not everyone was against Christ. They saw to it that the majority of the people with them before Pilate were on their side. It must have been a fickle mob who could be easily influenced either way. No doubt some of the same persons who had shouted "Hosanna to the King," when Jesus made His triumphal entry the Sunday before, now yelled, "Crucify Him" and followed Him eagerly to Golgotha. It is human nature to like cheap excitement and gory thrills.

Nobody showed pity when the Lord's exhausted body fell. No doubt several of Jesus' disciples were in the crowd along with some of His followers, but no one came forward to help Him up. Everyone was either too afraid or without pity. Furthermore, any Jew touching Jesus would become unclean because Jesus was bleeding and on the way to His execution. In the eyes of the Jews He was a condemned, unclean person.

The Roman soldiers pressed into service a man from Cyrene named Simon (Matthew 27:32) to carry the

Lord's cross bar. Cyrene was a city in Libya in North Africa and most likely Simon was a black man. What an honor God bestowed on the black race! A man from a faraway country helped the fainting Son of God carry the wood on which the Lamb of God would die.

The word for compelled in this instance is the Greek word *angaruo* which means to impress into service. In other words, Simon was not *forced* but *asked* to help and he agreed. Neither Roman nor Jewish law could make someone else carry a cross for a condemned person unless he agreed to it. Simon did and those laboring steps of his up to Golgotha must have done a great work for him. He beheld Jesus—and we find later that his family was counted among the believers. No doubt Simon himself became a follower of Jesus, perhaps that day (Mark 15:21; Romans 16:13). He couldn't help it. He watched Jesus walk to His death as a conqueror.

Rising to His feet after the heavy load was taken off His shoulders, Jesus stood and turned toward some weeping women in the crowd. Maybe they didn't dare to take His side in words, but they cried bitterly over Him. Jesus said tenderly and in deep compassion to them: "Daughters of Jerusalem, don't weep for Me but for yourselves and for your children" (Luke 23:28).

The Lord's inner eye looked down the corridor of time. Less than forty years later He saw how barren women, who by Jewish tradition were considered cursed by God, found themselves the fortunate ones. They didn't have to watch their children die when Jerusalem fell. Neither would they eat their own babies as some women did according to Josephus' description of the horrors of Jerusalem's seige by the Romans in A.D. 70. "If I, the living tree, an innocent man, suffer like this," Jesus said in prophetic foresight, "what will happen to you and the next generation who carry the guilt of murdering Me" (v. 31).

Even though the crowd cried out "May His blood come upon us and our children" (Matthew 27:25), Jesus, by His words, was not condemning the whole Jewish race for the actions of a few as many people have done. He simply was telling the people that they must take the consequences of their behavior.

Jesus' unselfish love turned His attention to other people even at a time when His body suffered so badly that He could hardly walk anymore. No doubt His heart ached more deeply than His back where the skin hung bleeding over raw open flesh.

Not only did Jesus sorrow for those weeping women but also for the whole Jewish nation—His own beloved people. He knew what would happen to them for thousands of years to come. They would wander spiritually blinded to the events they saw before their own eyes. Generation after generation would be without a homeland, without a hope, without a Messiah. Their rejection hurt Him deeper than when the nails were driven into His wrists.

The details of the method of Roman crucifixion was recently discovered when a skeleton was found during an archaeological digging in the Jewish quarter of the old city of Jerusalem. The prisoner's hands were nailed to the wood through the wrist. (In Jewish reckoning the hand extended from the tips of the fingers to the elbow, so the New Testament account of piercing His hands is still correct.) The cross bar was fastened to the upright beam which had a little shelf at the height of a man's hip. Upon this shelf the prisoner could hoist himself for brief periods under great pain. The feet were laid on top of each other and a single long spike fastened both heels to the cross. The cross itself was lifted by ropes and dropped into a hole dug for that purpose. Roman soldiers were not known for tenderness and consideration. They didn't care how badly a hanging, suffering body was jarred when the cross was finally dropped to a standing position.

What did Jesus think of when He uttered His first sentence after the cross stood up straight and the weight of His masculine body pulled on His nailed hands? "Father, forgive them for they don't know what they are doing," Jesus prayed, while perhaps the other two prisoners who were crucified with Jesus cursed and screamed in pain.

"Father, forgive *them*," He said. Did He mean the rough calloused Roman soldiers? Did He look at the Jewish leaders who watched the whole scene gleefully and without any human compassion? Or, did He mean not only the people who killed Him, but those who down the ages have rejected and denied His great sacrifice? Did He pray that prayer for you and me? For our sins also nailed Him to the cross so that we might live forever.

The Bible doesn't say, but my heart knows that His love embraced *all* of us, every human being who ever lived. No doubt the Father in heaven answered His Son's prayer and forgave *all* of us humans for killing His Son. No particular race or person shall ever be excluded from salvation because their forefathers killed Jesus Christ. The only thing God cannot forgive is the rejection of His Son. This *is* the unpardonable sin (John 3:36).

I wonder if the Jewish leaders or the Roman soldiers heard His beautiful prayer? Both groups were rather busy.

The Jews were greatly aggravated when the cross rose and they could read the sign Pilate had nailed above Jesus' head (John 19:19). It was customary for the Romans to record a prisoner's name, where he came from, the crime for which he had to die and then to display this record near the place of execution. No doubt all three crosses on Golgotha carried a sign that day. The Jews protested to Pilate about the way he described Jesus. In three languages—Hebrew (Aramaic) for the common people, Greek for the educated class, and Latin as the official Roman language—Pilate had inscribed: "Jesus of Nazareth, the King of the Jews" (John 19:19).

The Jews demanded a change of wording (v. 21). Pilate was greatly irritated. He knew they had tricked him into consenting to Jesus' death out of malice and jealousy, not because He deserved it. Also, Pilate wanted to teach the Jewish people a lesson: this punishment would happen to *anyone* who would try to become a king or leader of the Jewish nation. The crime he recorded was a slap at their Messianic hopes. "What I have written, I have written," Pilate snapped. "It stays exactly as it is" (v. 22).

It gauled and humiliated the Jews that Pilate would even dare indicate that their king could come from Nazareth. Their kings came from Bethlehem! It made their victory and triumph shallow that Jesus of Nazareth was declared one of their kings by Rome. But they couldn't change it, for even a higher authority than Pilate had ordained it—the God of heaven!

Meanwhile, the Roman soldiers passed their time gambling for the prisoners' possessions and clothing. They had to stay on watch to make sure Pilate's orders were carried out (vv. 23,24). So they divided the stuff into four piles except for Jesus' seamless robe. They didn't want to tear it so they gambled for it (John 19:24). With this action they fulfilled Old Testament prophecy and didn't even know it (Psalm 22:18).

Many others didn't hear the Lord's forgiving prayer, either. They were too busy laughing at Him: "So You said You can destroy the Temple and rebuild it in three days?" they teased. "Come down *if* You are the Son of God (Matthew 27:40).

"*If* You are the Son of God?" Jesus had heard those words before and He knew who spoke again through their human lips (Matthew 4:6). How He pitied those deceived, blinded people of His own race and how He loved them!

"He saved others," some leaders mocked, "but He cannot save Himself" (Matthew 27:42). What truth they spoke in jest and abuse, truth they couldn't see even while they said it.

Yes, Jesus could *not* save Himself and still save others and He knew it. In the Garden of Gethsemane, when His Father's cup trembled in His human hand for some agonizing moments, He decided *not* to save Himself so that He might save others. He permitted His enemies to fulfill His Father's plan of salvation, laid before the foundation of the earth (1 Corinthians 2:6-8).

Jesus' enemies thought they had finally gotten control over Him, but they never had less control than on the day when they finally managed to kill Him. They had schemed His death for two years but until "God's time" had come they couldn't do a thing (John 13:1). When they finally reached their goal, they congratulated themselves, but they didn't realize that they were tools of Satan, used in a great drama like puppets. And Satan ran the show *as God permitted it* so that evil would be triumphed over at the end.

Jesus was not only taunted by the people below Him but by one of the criminals who hung on a cross beside Him. "So, You're the Messiah, are You? Prove it by saving Yourself and us too while You're at it" (Luke 23:39).

The other criminal reproved him, "Don't you even fear God when you are dying? Look, we deserve to die but this man has done nothing wrong." Then he turned his head to Jesus. "Jesus," he said humbly, "remember me when You come into Your kingdom" (v. 42). We do not know how much that thief on the cross understood about Christ's mission. It is possible that he had heard Jesus speak before. Maybe he had watched His kingly dignity in the judgment hall of Pilate when all three were brought together to be led to their death.

Many Jews believed in resurrection; even the Pharisees did. This dying man believed that Jesus was the Son of God who would someday establish His kingdom and he wanted to be in it in his resurrected body.

What a bright moment for Jesus during a time of apparent total defeat and failure. Nobody else spoke up for Him. Some of His disciples were there but they didn't defend Him. They were crushed and didn't believe anymore that He was the Messiah. The dying thief was the first one to grasp in pain and confusion the one all-important truth: Jesus is the Saviour and I can ask for admission into His kingdom. He had no time to be baptized, join a church, pay tithe, or do the many other prerequisites some people think are necessary for salvation. All he could do was believe and ask!

He got a solemn assurance and needed no detailed explanation about the how and why. Jesus said: "Verily, I say unto thee, today shalt thou be with Me in paradise" (Luke 23:43). It was enough!

As Jesus' eyes looked down from His elevated position and recognized faces—He saw His mother and John, the disciple He loved. Jesus' concern was now directed toward the woman who had given Him birth and trained Him as a child. She was obviously a widow and the sons of His foster father, Joseph, didn't believe in Him at that point. "Woman," (a term of respect) Jesus said tenderly, "behold thy son." He turned His face to John, "Behold thy mother" (John 19:26,27).

Jesus, while hanging on the cross, had thoughts only for others who needed Him. He prayed for His enemies, assured a dying repentant thief of salvation and looked after His precious mother who needed a home. John took her to his home from that day on and looked after her like a son.

But Christ did more with His request. He made it clear that His mother had the same position in relation to Him as anyone else who loved Him, no special inroad, no extraordinary privileges. He made her John's mother before He died—and with that He broke the last human tie. He now had fulfilled all His responsibilities toward those who were around Him, and He could at last be alone with His Father.

A strange darkness fell over the entire land about noontime which lasted until 3:00 that afternoon (Mark 15:33). It wasn't an expected eclipse of the sun but a supernatural darkness that covered the hill of Golgotha and the whole area and, most likely, sent many onlookers home. For three hours nature veiled in utter darkness the suffering of three dying men who would, every so often, hoist themselves up on the little shelf to take some deep breaths before they let go again and hung limply.

Crucifixion is death by suffocation. When the body gets too exhausted to lift itself for breathing, the lungs collapse and the person suffocates. It is a long, slow and cruel death. History tells of people who did not die for several days. How long would it take for these three men to die? Jewish law would not allow a body to remain on a cross over the Sabbath (John 19:31).

About 3:00 in the afternoon, Jesus shouted: *Eloi, Eloi, lama sabachthani* which means "My God, My God, why have You forsaken Me" (Mark 15:34)? With darkness came the horrible separation Christ had dreaded in the Garden of Gethsemane. Never had He been separated from His heavenly Father. Even in the times of great earthly danger He could say, "I am not alone, My Father is with Me" (John 16:32).

Finally the time of the evening sacrifice at the Temple was at hand. Across the hill on the Temple Mount the passover lamb would be slain as a sacrifice at any moment. The slaying of God's lamb was at hand, too—and the Father had withdrawn His presence from His only beloved Son. Christ became sin and God cannot tolerate sin, not even when His own Son represents it.

The sinless One became cursed by God because He hung on a tree (Deuteronomy 21:23; Galatians 3:13). He had to die alone to redeem other people's sin. I believe that Christ could not see beyond the grave at the moment when He cried for God's presence. He did not know if He, as the sinbearer, would forever be separated from His Father. He only knew that it was God's will for Him to die in place of the human race. He did not even dare to call Him Father anymore. He knew how offensive sin was to a pure, sinless God. He addressed Him like the psalmist (Psalm 22:1).

People listened and said, "Is He calling for Elijah?" Jewish tradition had made Elijah the patron saint of pious men in their hour of great need. And the people wondered if Christ was finally calling for help. Some scoffers were still around. "Leave Him alone," they said to those who tried to give Him a drink. "Let's see whether Elijah will come and save Him!"

I wonder if perhaps Jesus heard the faint singing of the Temple choir as they celebrated the evening sacrifice and knew that His incredible suffering was coming to an end, also. There was one more prophetic word of Scripture to fulfill (Psalm 69:21).

"I am thirsty," He said (John 19:28). They dipped a sponge into vinegar and put it on a hyssop branch and held it to His mouth. He tasted it and said, with a loud voice, "It is finished!"

What did these three words mean? Did Jesus say that His suffering was done? No doubt this was included, but

He had finished so much more than that. These three words embraced the whole world and the universe.

If the earth was ever on display to the whole universe, it was, no doubt, on this day when Jesus died (1 Corinthians 4:9). I am sure the angels and all heaven watched the whole happening with breathless shock and wondered: would the earth creatures really *dare* to kill their Creator? The mystery which God kept secret for long ages was finally revealed (1 Corinthians 2:6-8). The lamb, which was slain long before the foundation of the earth was laid, was about to die (Revelation 13:8). The great conflict between Satan and God would be finished. (See, *I Am But a Child in Christ*, chapter 12). Satan would never again be able to convince any sinless creature of God that he (the devil) had a good program and kingdom. Satan's malice was revealed when he shoved his human servants to inhuman sadism and hate. He and his human helpers were so intent on trying to destroy the Son of God that they overlooked the fact that by so doing they fulfilled God's plan of salvation. And the three words, "It is finished" declared the end of Satan's power and the complete victory of God for the human race (1 Corinthians 15:55-57). Satan had lost his hold on the earth. Adam had sold out to him and the devil was the official "prince of the earth" after the fall (John 16:11), but now the promise given to Eve finally was fulfilled (Genesis 3:15).

The serpent bruised the Saviour's heel—literally—with a long spike but in doing so his head was crushed.

"It is finished," God's shout of victory, echoed through the entire universe. Jesus bought back the earth and it was His again, by creation and redemption (Colossians 1:16; Revelation 11:15).

"Father, into Thy hands I commend My spirit," Jesus cried out, and then He died.

The Gospel writers emphasize that Jesus spoke in a

loud voice before He gave up His ghost and died (Matthew 27:50; Mark 15:37; Luke 23:46). When a man is dying on a cross he is no longer able to shout or cry out loud. His lungs are collapsing and he gasps for air. The Jews and Romans knew that, for when they wanted to speed up the death of the other two criminals, they simply smashed their legs. From that moment on the dying man couldn't pull himself up anymore to breathe and soon he suffocated.

Christ was in full control and power up to the last moment.

I am convinced that just as the High Priest in the Temple ceremony stood on top of the steps and shouted, "Slay the lamb," Christ shouted His last words and died.

He gave up His spirit—nobody took it from Him, not even Satan. Jesus had said that He would lay His life down and take it up again (John 19:30).

When Christ knew that the circle was completed and the plan of redemption finished, He permitted Himself to be what He had been when He entered this earth, a little boy. At His mother's knees He had prayed the same words a hundred times. Just as an English-speaking child is taught to pray, "Now I lay me down to sleep," and a German child repeats, "Muede bin ich, geh zur Ruh," so every evening a Jewish child says the words of Psalm 31, verse 5: "Into Thy hands I commit my Spirit."

No doubt Jesus knew the whole Psalm, but these few words were enough to put Himself into God's hand. He called Him again, "Father," and in sublime submission and trust Jesus, in His last breath, put Himself into His Father's hands.

The Bible does not tell us the final cause of Jesus' death but John makes a special point to tell that when the Roman spear pierced His side blood and water flowed out (John 19:34). Medical science suggests that this was a sign that Jesus died from a physical rupture of the heart. I have no doubt that my Jesus died of a broken heart. What else could have killed Him but the burden of sin which crushed Him, and the terrible loneliness He suffered when His Father forsook Him? He could handle anything as long as His Father was with Him. When He hung between heaven and earth completely alone, while the powers of darkness veiled His future and tortured Him, Jesus still trusted God.

God the Father honored His Son's perfect submissiveness and trust. When the sun rose on the third day, it rose over a lone hill and an empty grave, for God had called His Son back to eternal life and His former glory. The circle had been completed, and IT WAS FINISHED!

LET'S PRAY: Dear Father in heaven, I want to thank You that You *gave* Your Son to die for us, the human race! The Bible does not tell too much about You while Your Son was condemned and crucified, but I know that You as a loving Father agonized with Your Son every step of the way, clear to the end! Even when You had to withdraw Your presence to permit Jesus to be the complete redemption for our sin, You suffered with Him. How can I ever thank You, oh Father, and You, my Jesus, for all You have done for me? Human words are far too poor to express my gratitude. It will take me all of eternity to thank and praise You enough. And I will do it forever. In Jesus' name. Amen.

26
FOLLOW ONLY ME

Between the time of the evening sacrifice and the beginning of the Sabbath stood three short hours. The Jews of Christ's time started every new day at 6:00 in the evening, regardless of when the sun set in order to reckon time. Jesus died around 3:00 in the afternoon or at the ninth hour (Matthew 27:46).

Many unusual happenings followed His death in short order. In the Temple the curtain secluding the Holy of Holies from the rest of the Temple tore from top to bottom, rent by unseen, supernatural power. No human hand could tear a heavy curtain from top to bottom against the weave. But the curtain did tear and behind it loomed an empty room (v. 51).

When Nebuchadnezzar took the people of Israel captive into Babylon, the Jews lost their most prized shrine, the Ark of the Covenant. With it they lost their mercy seat. Therefore they did not celebrate the Day of Atonement according to the Old Testament rules anymore, but they did keep many other feasts and religious activities which had become as empty as the room they kept hidden with a curtain. Now God tried again to send a message to the religious leaders, but they didn't understand the deep meaning.

An earthquake shook the earth and big rocks tumbled. Graves were opened and godly people of the past came back to life again and appeared to many (vv. 52, 53).

The captain of the Roman military unit handling

Jesus' execution observed everything and said in great awe, "Surely this Man was innocent; this was God's Son" (v. 54).

Many women had stayed close, those who had followed and ministered to the Master, and they didn't know what to do next. They just wept in deep sorrow (vv. 55,56). To the last moment, perhaps, Jesus' followers and friends hoped that something spectacular would happen. Now it was all over! He wasn't the Messiah after all, just a good, great idealistic Man who had lost out as so many on earth before Him had.

Joseph of Arimathea, a member of the Jewish supreme court who had been a secret disciple of Jesus for fear of the Jewish leaders, went now to Pilate and boldly asked for the body of Jesus. Pilate couldn't believe that Jesus was already dead but the Roman officer in charge confirmed the fact. And Pilate granted Joseph's request (vv. 57,58). So Joseph came and took away Jesus' limp body and Nicodemus, who had come to Jesus by night (see chapter 13), helped Joseph prepare the corpse for burial.

Both men were rich and influential and they used their influence and means to protect the body of Jesus. The Romans would have thrown Him into the Valley of Gehenna, on the garbage dump of the city. No doubt, the other two who were crucified went there.

After Jesus' body was wrapped in the customary way, with white, clean linen strips saturated with a hundred pounds of embalming ointments made from myrrh and aloes, He was buried in Joseph's brand new, unfinished sepulchre. All of this fulfilled prophecy (Isaiah 53:9).

The service of love had to be done in great haste for no decent Jew would dare break the Sabbath. The two godly men were already in bad shape because they had touched a dead person and therefore could not observe the Passover feast and the Feast of Unleavened Bread.

They would have to wait a month before they could re-celebrate (Numbers 9:10,11).

They laid Him into a grave which was very close to Golgotha and Joseph rolled a great stone in front of the entrance (Matthew 27:59,60). The women watched and wept and finally went home to prepare more spices for a proper embalming. However, they had to wait until the Sabbath was over before they could do anything more (Luke 23:55,56).

It seems that nobody had a good night's rest as quietness finally settled over the city. No doubt Jesus' followers went into deep mourning. It was the Jewish custom to mourn for a family member or friend at least seven days. During that time a man could neither wash nor anoint his head but showed by his disheveled appearance that he was distraught and sad. The disciples must have been in utter confusion and also in great fear for their lives. It was usually the Roman custom to kill the followers with the leader.

The women wept until they could weep no more trying to understand what had gone wrong. There seemed to be no ray of hope anywhere.

The chief priests and Pharisees must not have slept well either. Something gnawed at the pit of their stomachs and they couldn't relax or enjoy to the fullest their victory over the Galilean upstart. They remembered some words Jesus had said and they had reason to believe them. So they broke some more of their Jewish laws when they went to Pilate the next day. They broke the Sabbath to find peace of mind (Matthew 27:62).

"Sir," they said, "that liar once said He'll come back to life after three days. Please seal the tomb and put some soldiers before it so the disciples cannot come and steal His body and tell a wild story" (vv. 63,64).

Pilate disliked these men as much as they disliked him in normal times. "You have your own watch," Pilate said, "Go your way and make it as sure as you possibly can. Keep Him in" (v. 65).

So, in spite of the Sabbath day, they made the sepulchre sure, sealed the stone with the Roman seal on both sides and set up men to watch that nobody came near the tomb.

Finally they had Him put away for good and He couldn't come out even if He were alive and tried. How could one man roll away such a big stone especially from the inside? He would have to stay in the hewed out tomb to rot—they'd see to it!

The Temple service began every morning before sunrise. A priest climbed the pinnacle of the Temple while the choir and the various priests in charge waited. As soon as the man on top of the wall saw the first rays of the sun, he called out, "The sun has risen."

The priest in charge called back, "Does it shine as far as Hebron?" (In other words, "Are you sure it's not just a reflection?")

The man on top said, "Yea, it shines as far as Hebron."

Upon that answer the priest in charge commanded, "Open the gates and slay the lamb!"

The worshipers then entered and the morning service began.

I have no doubt in my mind that the resurrection of Jesus happened during the time of this service on the first day of the week.

An angel from heaven came down just before sunrise and the earth shook with a great earthquake while he rolled the tomb stone away and sat on it.

And when the priest on top of the wall called back, "The sun has risen," I can see the Son of God rise and come out of the tomb!

The priest asked, "Does it shine as far as Hebron?"

and I am sure an angelic choir in heaven rejoiced in ecstasy, "Yea, as far as the ends of the earth!"

The guards had fainted in fear and when they came back to consciousness they staggered toward the city and found the high priest. They had a story to tell and they told it. After all, they could be punished severely unless they proved that what happened was beyond their control.

Meanwhile some other things happened at the empty tomb. The women had made their way to the tomb very early in the morning. They carried ointments to embalm their Master properly and must have gotten there just around sunrise. They had been wondering who would roll the big stone away for them. They didn't know about the sealed tomb and the watch guards for they had stayed quietly at home and kept the Sabbath according to the laws of their day.

When they arrived they found the stone removed and the tomb open. Mary Magdalene gave one look and ran back to the city to tell Peter and John (John 20:1,2).

The other women went into the tomb and found it empty. The precious body was gone! They puzzled and wondered what could have happened when two shimmering angels stood before them and said, "Why do you look for Someone in a tomb when He is alive! Can't you remember what He told you before He was crucified? Go and tell the disciples, including Peter. Jesus is going ahead of you to Galilee. He'll meet you there" (Matthew 28:7).

The women turned and ran, badly frightened but filled with a new joy. Of course, they remembered now! They hurried back to the city to find the disciples and give them the angel's message.

Meanwhile Mary Magdalene found Peter and John and reported that the body of Christ had been taken out of the tomb (John 20:2). The two men ran to the tomb to see for themselves. John got there first and looked in but he didn't enter. He waited for Peter (John 20:4-6). It seems that Simon Peter was the older of the two and John respected him as his elder and let him walk in first. They both found the rolled grave cloth and face covering in a separate place. It looked just as though a person had awakened and slipped out of his sleeping covers, leaving them in place. The two men remembered Christ's words and believed. They left the empty tomb and went home.

Mary came back to the tomb after Peter and John left and cried her heart out. She stooped and searched every corner of the burial place but it was empty. Two angels whom she thought were men sat at the head and foot of the place where the body of Jesus had lain. They asked, "Why are you crying?"

"Because they have taken away my Lord," Mary sobbed. She glanced over her shoulder and saw a man behind her, too (vv. 11-15).

"Why are you crying?" He asked. "Who are you looking for?"

She thought He was the gardener. "Sir," she said urgently, "if You have taken Him away, tell me where You have put Him and I will go and get Him."

"Mary," Jesus said. She turned toward Him.

"Master," she cried out and most likely threw herself down to embrace or kiss His feet as she had done before. Nobody could say, "Mary," with so much love and tenderness as Jesus did. She knew it was Jesus by the way He called her name. She reached out and held on to Him. She simply would never let Him get away again but would stay with Him wherever He went.

"Don't cling to Me," Jesus said gently, "for I haven't yet ascended to the Father. Now go and tell My brothers ... (v. 17).

The first person Jesus appeared to and spoke to was

Mary Magdalene the woman from whom He had cast out seven demons (Luke 8:2). He not only honored a woman with His first appearance but He made her the messenger to His disciples (John 20:18).

The second appearance was again to a group of women and again He told them to carry His message to His eleven disciples (Matthew 28:9,10).

Of course the disciples didn't believe them. It sounded like a fairytale to their rational minds and who could trust the tales of women (Mark 16:11)?

Two disciples decided to leave the city and go back to their home in the village of Emmaus, seven miles out of Jerusalem. All they could talk about was the death of Jesus. A stranger joined them and entered their discussion. He explained patiently and in detail why the Messiah had to die and rise from the dead, quoting passage after passage from the Scriptures. When they arrived at home they invited Him to stay. Not until He asked God's blessing on the food, broke the bread and handed it to them did they recognize that it was Jesus Himself.

The Bible does not tell us how they finally recognized Him. Did they notice the nail scars on His wrists? Did He pray in a certain way that was most typical of Jesus? They recognized Him—and He disappeared. The two disciples returned at once in the deep of night to Jerusalem to tell the others, but they knew already.

Jesus had obviously appeared to Peter sometime that day or evening, too (Luke 24:34).

While the disciples talked Jesus suddenly stood among them and greeted them. But they were terribly frightened. They thought He was a ghost (Luke 24:37). He showed them His hands and feet and they still couldn't believe that He had a body and was not a spirit only. Jesus finally asked, "Do you have anything to eat?" They gave Him a piece of broiled fish and He ate it as they watched Him. This thoughtful gesture of Jesus not only showed them that His body could eat and digest but it proved to them beyond a doubt that He was still their friend. In Middle East custom only friends share food with each other.

One of the disciples, Thomas, the twin, was not with the group during Jesus' visit. When the disciples saw Thomas again, they told him, "We have seen the Lord."

Thomas insisted, "I won't believe it unless I see the nail wounds in His hands and put my fingers into them and place my hand into His side (John 20:24,25).

Eight days later the disciples were together again and this time the twin, Thomas, was with them. The men kept the doors locked. They were still greatly concerned about their safety. The Jewish leaders hadn't changed their hostile attitude yet. But, as before, Jesus suddenly stood among them and greeted them.

Without reproach He turned to Thomas, held up His hands and said kindly, "Thomas, put your finger into My scars, your hand into My side. Don't be without faith any longer. Only believe" (v. 27).

Thomas looked at Jesus and felt overwhelmed, "My Lord and my God," he said reverently (v. 28).

Jesus said, "You believe because you had a chance to see Me. But blessed are those who did not and will not be able to see Me but believe anyway" (v. 29).

Did Jesus think of you and me and the many generations after who had to believe by hearing and reading only? He blessed us with a special blessing.

Jesus appeared in many places and at different times. Some of the happenings are not described in detail in the Gospels. Not everything about Jesus could be told by the Bible writers for a thousand books could not hold the whole story (John 21:25).

Paul makes reference to several appearances. On one occasion Jesus was seen by more than five hundred people at the same time (1 Corinthians 15:6).

Jesus showed Himself enough to dispel the doubts of His followers and to disprove the wild stories told by the Jewish leaders and the men who had watched the tomb. These had been bribed with money and told what to say by the high priest himself. "While the watchmen slept at night, the disciples came and stole the body," they said (Matthew 28:13-15).

What an admission of defeat. Watchmen knew better than to sleep on duty. Furthermore how could they know what happened if they were sleeping? And if they saw the disciples roll away the big stone (the noise would have awakened at least one of the watching men), they would have stopped them for sure. Lies always have very short legs, and cannot run very far without being detected. The story of the sleeping watchmen must have been a great embarrassment to everyone concerned, but it was better than to admit that Jesus had risen in power and glory.

Jesus appeared not only to bring proof upon proof that He was truly alive again, but He did so to prepare His followers for a future without Him. Jesus knew that His return to heaven was imminent and He had to reassure and teach His disciples many things before He left. One of the most touching stories of the risen Lord's tender teaching is found in the last chapter of the Gospel of John.

The disciples had made their way to Galilee. They had been told to meet the Lord there (Matthew 28:7; Mark 16:7). It seemed natural for the fishermen to wait for the Lord at the lake. They were a group of seven (John 21:2) and Peter said to the others, "I'm going fishing."

Did he get impatient waiting for the Lord? When their funds ran out, did they need a good catch to make ends meet?

The Bible does not tell us but we know that they did

not catch anything and came toward the shore at dawn with empty boats.

They saw a figure standing on the beach in the first light of day but they couldn't recognize Him. "Did you catch anything, lads?" the Man asked.

"No," the tired discouraged men answered. They were hungry, too, after a long night of fishing for nothing.

"Throw out your net on the right side of the boat and you'll catch plenty of fish," the Man suggested.

Did the first trace of recognition light up in the heads of the disciples when they heard these words? Did Peter remember another time when he was told to fish against all principles of fishing?

When the Man said, "Throw your net on the right side of the boat," He asked for something unusual. The nets were customarily lowered on the left side and hauled in with strong right arms. Only a left-handed man would want to fish from the right side of the boat. Perhaps Peter remembered the time on the lake when Jesus suggested that they go fishing by day—and out in the deep, too (Luke 5:4). When the sun shines on the clear waters of the Sea of Galilee, the fish go to the bottom of the lake. There is no net big enough to reach that low. The only way to fish by day on the Sea of Galilee is with a fishing line near the edge of the lake, since some of the fish will feed and hide in the rushes of the shore during the day.

Peter had obeyed the suggestion and so many fish were caught that the net broke. The disciples didn't argue this morning either. They did as they were told. The net started to pull with heavy weight. They had made a large haul.

John's heart skipped a beat. "Peter," he said, "that's the Lord" (John 21:7).

Peter did what came natural to him. Impulsive, fervent, impetuous and loving, he wanted to see the Master. So he jumped out of the boat. But first to be properly dressed he put on his tunic and then he waded to shore.

The others stayed in the boat and did the work at hand. They dragged the net for three hundred feet to shore and counted the big fish. They caught 153! What a catch and the net didn't even tear (v. 11).

What a welcome sight and smell greeted them when they came out of the water, shivering a bit and in need of breakfast. A warm fire had been kindled by the Stranger and fish were broiling over it while some bread toasted (v. 9). Would the resurrected Lord and King of the universe build a little fire with His own hands and prepare breakfast for some lonely fishermen? Indeed He would!

"Bring some of the fish you caught," the Lord said. Seven hungry fishermen could eat a lot. They brought the fish and the Master served His seven friends breakfast. He ate too (v. 12,13).

The Bible indicates that it was a very quiet meal. Nobody dared to ask questions (v. 12). Seven men stared into the dying embers of a smoldering fire while they ate and battled with remorse and guilt.

Peter remembered another fire in Caiaphas' courtyard, the crowing of a cock and Jesus' long loving look before he, Peter, ran out the gate to weep in self-disgust and helpless repentance (Luke 22:54-62).

Thomas sat and heard himself insist over and over, "I will not believe unless I *see* with my own eyes." And he remembered what Jesus said when he "saw," "Blessed are those who don't need to see and still believe (John 20:24-29).

Nathaniel recalled his arrogant words, "What good can come from Nazareth?" And when Jesus was introduced to him and said, "Behold an Israelite indeed in whom there is no guile," Nathaniel didn't say humbly,

"Thank You, Sir, for Your high opinion of me, but I am not *that* good!" Instead he had asked in utter conceit: "Whence knowest Thou me" (John 1:45-48)?

James and John sat and remembered the many times they had acted like "the sons of thunder" instead of being true followers of Jesus (Mark 3:17). They had always been so eager to revenge, to call fire from heaven and to act like big shots. They had even been very unfair and sent their mother to secure for themselves the highest positions beside Jesus in His kingdom (Matthew 20:20,21).

We don't know what remorse the other two disciples, whom John doesn't name, carried, but no doubt all seven of them felt terrible about something they hadn't done right. After all, they *all* forsook Him when He was arrested (Mark 14:50).

I have no doubt but that every disciple had the same desire and similar thoughts. "If I only could go back and start all over! This time I would do it *right*. I would never betray, deny, question or argue with Him ever again! I would trust Him for what He is, not for what He does according to my demands! Oh, if I only could erase my embarrassing mistakes of the past and start anew!"

After the meal Jesus looked lovingly into Peter's face and addressed him because he so often was the spokesman for the whole group.

In order to get the deep meaning of the following conversation we must understand the three Greek words describing love. The Greek language calls love either *eros* (physical infatuation), *phileo* (reactive, brotherly or friendship love) or *agape* (the love of God as expressed in action, principle and by will—love for love's sake). (See, *I Am But a Child in Christ*, chapter 43.)

"Simon, son of John," Jesus said, "do you love Me more than these others?"

What did Jesus mean with these few words? Jesus called Peter by his full family name, recognizing his respectable Jewish heritage and suggesting that he hadn't yet become what He had in mind for him to become—a rock for God's kingdom. "Simon," Jesus suggested tactfully, "remember the time when you said that even if all the others forsake Me, you would stay true and stand by? Do you still believe you can do *more* than the other disciples? Do you *agape* me more than these?"

Simon Peter's self-confidence had dwindled to nothing. He knew himself a lot better now than when he had made such bragging statements a few weeks ago. He looked humbly into his Master's face and said, "Yes, Lord, You know that I love [*phileo*] You. I am Your friend" (John 21:15).

Simon admitted that he didn't love Jesus as he once thought he did. He had only human love for Jesus, which could let him be scared, run away and deny Jesus in time of pressure.

Jesus looked at Peter and said kindly, "Tend My lambs." With it He said, "Though you have less to give than you thought and I hoped for, I entrust My new flock of coming believers into your hands. Look after the children, but especially the *new babes* in Christ. They need your loving patience, care and understanding. You know better than anyone how often babes fall down."

Next Jesus simplified His question. "Simon," He repeated, "son of John, do you love [*agape*] Me?" With it Jesus asked, "Do you have any *agape* love for Me at all?"

A humbled, honest Peter said again, "Yes, Lord, You know I am Your *friend*. I *phileo* You (v. 16).

Jesus said, "I will take what you have. I trust you. Take care of My sheep. Lead My church."

A third time Jesus asked the same question, but this time He changed the word love from *agape* to *phileo*. He said, "Simon, son of John, do you really (and at least) *phileo* Me? Are you *really* My friend" (v. 17)?

Peter felt heartsick. Not only did he realize that Jesus had asked three times to remind him of his three denials, but Jesus had even questioned his human love as a friend. Grief-stricken but still humble and without trying to defend his action, Peter said quietly, "Lord, You *know* my heart; You know that I at least have *phileo* for You. I love You as much as I am capable of at this present moment."

Jesus nodded. Yes, He knew Peter's impulsive, honest, over-eager, temperamental heart. "Tend My little sheep." Jesus commissioned Him at last. The Lord laid on Peter the care of the most difficult group in the future church. Little sheep have outgrown the lamb stage, but are not yet mature adults with good wool, or able to bear lambs. They are in a transition period which renders them useless for awhile to the shepherd. Our society would call them "teenagers." Teenagers are not only the physically young teens but the Christians who are outgrowing their first love and baby stage in Christ and have begun to mature into spiritual adulthood. The transition period can often render them most obnoxious. They have *all* the answers, cause much turmoil and rebellion in a church and try the patience of any church elder or leader.

When Jesus entrusted even *that* flock into Peter's hands and into the hands of the other disciples, He said, "I trust you, even with the most impossible task. Though you don't have *My* love [*agape*] and patience yet, I know you'll get them in the future. I know you worry about the past and what you *don't* have, but I have *no* concern about that. All I know and care about is what you *do* have, *now!*

"Don't think of the past any more. I took care of it at the cross. Remember that I can handle your denials, mistakes and disobedience. My blood erases your *entire* past! I have forgotten it. All I long for is your love. And even if it isn't the true, full love yet, as long as you give Me *all* you have, it is enough for Me. I trust you, even if you and your love are not perfect. I take what you have at any given moment and I use what you are willing to give Me. Love will grow—and so will your service for Me. Just love Me!"

"Feed My little sheep," Jesus said to Peter, who was perhaps at that moment still a bit of a little sheep himself. But Jesus could look ahead and know how Simon Peter would mature and become so full of *agape* love for the Lord someday that he would fearlessly die on a cross. Jesus told him how he would die (John 21:18,19). Tradition tells us that Peter was crucified in Rome. He begged to be turned upside down on his cross for he didn't feel worthy to die the same way His Saviour did.

We do not know if Peter understood fully what Jesus meant when He spoke to him for the last time on the Sea of Galilee, but Jesus made one thing clear to Peter before He left: it was time for Peter and the rest of the disciples to stop worrying about the future of any of the other disciples, be it out of genuine concern, jealousy or other motive (v. 21).

"What is it to you what happens to John?" Jesus said to ever-eager Peter when, right after this significant talk, Simon Peter asked another one of his impulsive demanding questions. "Don't worry about others. *You follow Me!*"

These words must have rung in the hearts of Peter and the other disciples for the rest of their lives.

Forty days after Christ's resurrection His followers watched Jesus ascend into the sky and disappear in a cloud (Acts 1:9,10). He returned to the place He had come from thirty-three years ago: His Father's heaven. Jesus had prepared the hearts of those He left behind with many tender words. But nothing comforted them more than when He said, "Though I have to leave you bodily, you can be sure of this, I AM with you always, even to the end of the world (Matthew 28:20). Jesus in His new glorified body had not forgotten the terrible loneliness which had crushed Him on the cross. He said, "Because I was *all* alone, once without even My Father, you'll *never* have to be. I suffered it for you and I promise you, I'll never let you go through the same agony, ever! I shall always be with you and My Holy Spirit will come and fill you. So go and tell everybody the good news: I'll come back someday and take you home! Until then trust Me, love Me, and follow Me—and only Me!"

LET'S PRAY: Dear Jesus, words are too poor to express what's in my heart right now. I am one of Your disciples sitting at the fire and longing to start all over again. I have made so many mistakes. I know I did all the foolish things of everyone combined in Your little group. But it's not possible to go back and undo my failures.

I thank You that I don't have to. You took care of my past and *all* my sins and I can start *now* with a clean new leaf and forget the past.

Jesus, I do love You. I don't know how much, but I love You as much as I am capable of right now. You said that it is all You want. So take me as I am and let me do what I want to do most: to follow You, now and forevermore. Amen.

BIBLIOGRAPHY

Ausubel, Nathan, ed. *A Treasury of Jewish Folklore.* New York: Crown Publishers, Inc., 1948.

Cohen, Rev. Dr. A., ed. *The Soncino Books of the Bible,* 14 vols. London: The Soncino Press, 1947.

Cornfeld, Gaalyahu, ed. *Pictorial Bible Encyclopedia.* Tel Aviv: Hamikra Baolam Pub. House, Ltd., 1964.

Glatzer, Nahum N., ed. *The Passover Haggadah.* New York: Schocken Books, 1953, 1969.

Gross, William, J., ed. *Herod the Great.* Baltimore: Helicon Press, 1962.

The Jerusalem Post

Jeremias, Joachim. *Jerusalem in the Times of Jesus.* Philadelphia: Fortress Press, 1967.

Josephus, Flavius. *The Antiquities of the Jews.* Grand Rapids: Krogel Publications, 1960.

Josephus, Flavius. *The Wars of the Jews.* Grand Rapids: Krogel Publications, 1960.

Kittel, Gerhard, ed. *Theological Dictionary of the New Testament,* 10 vols. Grand Rapids: Wm. B. Eerdmans Publishing Company, 1964, 1976.

Roth, Cecil and Wigoder, Geoffrey, eds. *The New Standard Jewish Encyclopedia.* Garden City, NY: Doubleday and Company, Inc., 1970.

Vine, W. E. *An Expository Dictionary of New Testament Words.* Old Tappan, NJ: Fleming H. Revell Company, 1940.

Werblowsky, R. J. Zwi and Wigoder, Geoffrey, eds. *The Encyclopedia of Jewish Religion.* New York: Holt, Rinehart and Winston, Inc., 1965.